Rufus Putnam, Isaac J Finley

Pioneer record and reminiscences of the early settlers and

settlement of Ross County, Ohio

Rufus Putnam, Isaac J Finley

Pioneer record and reminiscences of the early settlers and settlement of Ross County, Ohio

ISBN/EAN: 9783337712006

Printed in Europe, USA, Canada, Australia, Japan

Cover: Foto ©ninafisch / pixelio.de

More available books at **www.hansebooks.com**

PIONEER RECORD

AND

REMINISCENCES

OF THE

EARLY SETTLERS AND SETTLEMENT

OF

ROSS COUNTY, OHIO.

—

By ISAAC J. FINLEY AND RUFUS PUTNAM.

CINCINNATI:
PRINTED FOR THE AUTHORS BY ROBERT CLARKE & CO.
1871.

PREFACE.

In endeavoring to accomplish faithfully what is contained in this work, it has been found that notwithstanding its narrow scope, it has involved considerable time, expense, labor, and difficulties, visiting, as we have, all the most noted forts, circles, mounds, camps, caves, cliffs, etc., within the county. We have endeavored to portray the toils, hardships, and privations of a pioneer life, when nothing but dense deep forests, inhabited only by wild, ferocious beasts, and bloody savages, covered the land : when the only habitation was the rude wigwam of the aborigines; when the howl of wolves, and scream of panthers, the hum of wild bees, the hissing and rattle of the poisonous snake, the gobble of the wild turkey, and the shrill whistle of the red hunter, constituted all the music that broke the solemn stillness of the backwoods. The first brave and hardy pioneers lived to see those forests melt away before the tide of industry, and fields of golden grain spring up to adorn the efforts of the husbandman with abundant harvests. Alas! those pioneers, the brave, enterprising men who made their homes first in the western land, with few exceptions, have passed away. Their names, at least, should be remembered by those who now reap the fruits of their labors.

CONTENTS.

PIONEER RECORD

OF

ROSS COUNTY, OHIO.

Introduction.

A few still live who were among the first pioneers of this neighborhood. They, perhaps, are the only ones who can fully appreciate the early home life among these hills and valleys. Only those who first cleared off these rough and sterile hills, who erected the first rough cabins, with their clapboard or bark roofs and puncheon floors, with blankets and quilts for doors and oiled paper for window-glass, with chimneys built of split sticks and mud, often not higher than their heads, can now, by contrast, value properly the comforts of a good modern home. Only those who have grubbed the thick underbrush and saplings; who have used the ax in deadening and felling the heavy timber, the maul and wedge in making the first rails; who have chopped up the trees, piled the brush, and then been smoked almost blind while burning the logs and brush, with fingers and hands bruised and burned, and arms begrimed with smoke and dust, and clothes torn from their backs, can have any idea of the pleasure there is in contemplating a beautiful, smooth lawn, without a stump or log. None but those who have held the first plow, amid roots, stumps, stones, and trees, while the faithful team was pulling and jerking it along, with the roots breaking and flying back against the plowman's shins, beating and bruising them from the knees down, can really enjoy the delight that this same plowman feels while holding the plow as it moves slowly along, turning the soil up to the genial rays of the sun, without a root or stump to obstruct it. Only those who have struggled for scanty crops among these clearings and upon the rough and sterile hill-sides, can properly estimate the tilling of the same fields of later years. Only those who have had to convey little sacks of corn on horseback, over winding cow-paths, along the sides of the hills, across the ravines and valleys, to the mill, there to wait for his grist, in order that his family might have some hasty-pudding for their evening meal, can appreciate the variety of bread, the abundance of bread material, and the conveniences of mills in our land. The little boy, often less than ten years old, would frequently, while going up the steep banks, feel his sack slipping from under him, or hanging too heavily on one side, and then he felt desolate enough. Many such calamities these little pioneers had to meet. The writer of this sketch, even in his day, has experienced several such mishaps on the way to mill, and sometimes had to wait for hours on the road, until some one came along and assisted in replacing the sack.

Mills were sometimes out of the question, and then the mortar and pestle would have to be resorted to. This was one of the most primitive articles of the country, and was made in the most primitive style. A log of some hard timber, about four feet long, and twenty inches in diameter, was squared at both ends; one end rested on the ground, while upon the other a small fire was kindled, so as to burn deepest into the center. In this way a cavity was formed, called a mortar, sufficient to hold a peck of corn. Then with a pestle, made heavy by attaching thereto an iron wedge, the corn was beaten until the bran or hull came off. This process was assisted by adding a little scalding water from time to time. After it became thoroughly dry, and the bran was blown away, this hominy, by being well cooked, made an excellent substitute for bread.

None but those who were deprived of an education by the want of a common school system can realize the great benefit of our popular mode of instruction. Our pioneers had no school system, and many of them hardly knew what a school was. The children of the present day, who now have comfortable school-houses and good teachers, and all provided at the public expense, have but little idea of the desolation and ignorance which prevailed prior to the commencement of our great common school system.

The territory now forming Ross county was well timbered at the time of its first settlement, abounding in the usual variety and extent of forest trees—the sugar, beech, hickory, walnut, poplar, and the oak of the different varieties, being the principal. The soil in places is very good; the larger proportion, however, is hilly and not very productive, but is very well adapted to the growing of fruit, grapes, etc., and the citizens, of later years, have turned their attention to the raising of fruit. One can scarcely pass a farm but he sees orchards and vineyards being set out, and some of them are quite extensive.

Huntington Township.

Present Civil Officers of Township.

Justices of the Peace, I. J. Finley, Samuel Rinehart, and A. J. Pummell; Trustees, Joseph Ringer, Samuel Rinehart, and Joseph Grubb; Treasurer, William Combs; Clerk, Jno. W. Kellough; Constables, William Wilson and John Lee; Land Appraiser, Thomas DeLong. Post-office, Hoopole, at Farmersville.

Huntington has never furnished any county officers under its present organization, except I. J. Finley, who represented, in part, Ross County in the Ohio Legislature in 1868–9; and it has never had a representative in the State's prison, I believe.

In McIntosh's Memoirs in 1789, page 13.

Daniel Boone encamped on Paint creek, September 7, 1789, near the Rock rapids, on his route from Manchester to Fort Clark, on Mad river. Gen. Putnam, on April 15th of the same year, encamped at the same place, on his route to Vincennes to treat with the Indians.

Old Pioneers.

John Cochenour, stone-mason, was in the war of 1812, now dead. Mr. Cochenour was of great service to the new settlers in building chimneys for their cabins, etc. One evening, while coming home from his work, he was belated and it grew very dark; when within a mile from home, five large wolves attacked him, and he having left his gun at home was forced to take shelter in a large dogwood tree that stood near his path, and there remain until the morning light drove his adversaries away.

Peter Streevey emigrated to Ohio at an early day from Pennsylvania; was in the war of 1812 as teamster; now dead; was a resident of Huntington township over sixty years; was a great hunter. He and a Mr. Rolston, of whom mention will be made in another place, started out with their guns and dogs one morning on a bear hunt. After being out for some time, being near what is called the Bald Knob, they heard the dogs barking, and going up to them they found them barking up a large chesnut tree which had been broken off at the top, leaving the stump some forty or fifty feet high and hollow at the top, and about twenty feet up there was another hole in the side of the stump. The two hunters thumped the tree with the butts of their guns, when a bear stuck his head out and Streevey fired, and the bear fell back into the stump. Streevey, supposing the bear dead, and being a good climber, climbed up the stump, taking with him a stout pole which he tied to his body with his suspenders, and upon arriving at the top commenced thrusting his pole down on the bear, when, to his surprise, bruin ran up and out at the top and down one side and Streevey on the other; the dogs met him at the foot of the tree, and one large dog of Streevey's locked jaws with the bear, and Streevey, in the excitement, fired at the bear, but only wounded him. He hastily reloaded his gun and snapped, but his gun being of the flint lock, as all were in those days, the powder being damp, his gun missed fire, when he renewed the priming and killed the bear; after which, he reascended the stump and found two cubs, which they killed. During their day's hunting they killed seven bears, among them a very large one, which had taken shelter behind the roots of a large white oak tree which had been blown down. Mr. Streevey, during his lifetime, killed a great many deer, wolves, turkeys, etc. When young he married a Miss Tabitha Thomas, whose father emigrated to Ohio in very early times, and lived for a short time in Chillicothe with his family, when but two or three log cabins had been built in the place. One day, Mrs. Streevey, when nine or ten years old, was left with her sister in charge of the cabin, near the banks of the Scioto river, while their mother went to the river to wash their clothing. Several Indians came into the cabin and commenced cutting off slices of venison, which they found hanging up, and roasting it on the coals. The two young girls became frightened and ran under the bed; but after awhile they thought it would not do to let the redskins eat all their meat, so slipping out from their hiding-place, they ran down to their mother and informed her of what was going on; whereupon the mother started for the house accompanied by a neighbor woman by the name of McMahan, I believe. On their way they armed themselves with clapboards, such as were used in those days for roofing. On entering the cabin they commenced clearing it of its intruders by lustily applying the boards to the naked backs of the redskins, which soon made them retreat in haste. Father Streevey and wife lived to a good old age, and died lamented and beloved by all who knew them.

Robert Bishop's Reminiscences.

Robert Bishop emigrated to Ohio from Berkeley county, Virginia, in 1805, by land, in wagons; has been a resident of Huntington township sixty four years; still living; was in the war of 1812 under Capt. George Yoakem; was second sergeant of his company; enlisted after Hull's surrender. The company went through Upper Sandusky; belonged to the brigade of Gen. E. Tupper; he received for his services forty acres of land. When they first encamped, while their captain was gone to report, one of their men went out to cut poles to build a tent; there was, a short distance from where they commenced to pitch their tents, a horse company encamped, and this man went on the grounds of the horse company, claimed and cut a pole, when he was arrested by them and put under guard; they had him under a large oak tree and guarded by several men with their horse-pistols. When Capt. Yoakem returned, he asked Mr. Bishop what that meant, seeing the men standing around the tree with their pistols in hand. Mr. Bishop told the captain they had one of his men under arrest. When Yoakem heard this he drew his sword

and ordered Bishop and another of his men to arm themselves
with their guns and follow him, which they did; they marched
boldly up to where the man was under the tree, the guards
standing around him with pistols in hand; Yoakem marched
through the guards and taking the prisoner by the arm told
him to go with him. The officers of the horse company ordered
the arrest of the captain, which he soon found out, when he drew
his men into line and ordered them to load their pieces. When
the horse company saw the hostile appearance of Capt Yoakem's company they drew back, and so the matter ended.

Mr. Bishop relates another incident connected with his soldier life. One day several of the horse company started out on
a reconnoitering expedition, and did not return until late in the
night; sometime during the night some of the horses breaking
loose from their riders, came dashing into camp, whereupon the
whole camp was aroused; a squad of the remaining company
mounted their steeds, snatched their arms, which were stacked
near by, and, loading them with buckshot, some having five or
six shot in them, started out to look after the party which
had not returned. Before going far, they met them returning,
when they all came in together, the men restacking their arms.
On the next morning one of the men was cleaning his gun; Mr.
Bishop and another of the company were standing near by,
when he snapped it, the gun went off, the contents passing between Mr. Bishop and the other soldier, whose name is forgotten,
so close they both felt the wind of the balls as they passed, and
striking a man standing near, killed him instantly, two balls
passing through his body, and breaking the leg of another man
named Hill, I believe.

Mr. Bishop was a home hunter, and helped to kill many
bears and wolves; was justice of the peace for many years,
besides holding several other township offices.

Henry Bishop, father of Robert, emigrated to Ohio at the
same time with Robert; purchased land in Huntington township in 1806, and died in 1820, at the age of ninety-eight.
Jacob and George Vincentheller were old hunters. Paul Stree-

vey was in the Revolutionary war. David and Jacob Toops were both in the war of 1812. John Lewis and George Vincentheller were the first settlers on what is known as the Alum Cliffs. John Methias was justice of the peace and county commissioner, in the first organization of the township, for some time. John Scantlin was in the Indian war of 1791, under Gen. St. Clair. John Yoakem was under Gen. Tupper, in the war of 1812. Job Haynes and George Grove were in the war of 1812, under Capt. William Keyes, of Huntington township, and were in Hull's surrender. Henry Long was sergeant in Capt. Elliott's home company. David Elliott was also in the war of 1812. George Ruffner, whose biography will appear in another place, was in the war of 1812; was a great Indian fighter, and was in Hull's surrender. George Houseman was in the war of 1812, and under Hull at the time of his surrender. Stanley Seymore was in the Indian war of 1791. Daniel Toops was in the war of 1812; weaver by trade, and farmer; now dead. David Shoemaker was in the war of 1812, under Capt. Keyes. Daniel Grubb was in the war of 1812; was a home hunter; killed several bears on his farm during his lifetime; lived to be very old; was an excellent farmer and a good citizen.

List of Old Pioneers furnished by Mrs. Mary W. Finley.

Isaac Jordan, in war of 1812; now dead. Richard Elliott emigrated from Ireland at an early day, and settled in the township; was in war of 1812; a weaver by trade. William Sadler. Jacob Seeleg was in war of 1812; started to go as substitute, but on arriving at Chillicothe the man he was going for had obtained some one in his place, when he volunteered in Captain Keyes' company, but, being a good gunsmith, was detailed to work at that business. Alex. Monroe. Henry Wilt was in the war of 1812; still living; wagon-maker by trade. Richard Honold, Thos. McCann, George Meyers, in the war of 1812 as teamsters; all dead. David Shotts, William McCann, Jos. Offort, Sr., Martin Howard, Nancy Park, John McCalley, David Murphy, Jacob Maurey, Peter Lightle (who served many years as

justice of the peace, and in other township offices), Frederick
Baker, John Kilbourne, Peter Stagner, Michael Thomas (was
an early settler, and a great hunter, in connection with Peter
Streevey and Benjamin Rolston, whose names appear in another
place in this work). Henry Miskel, an old colored man, was
among the first settlers, and deserves some notice. He rendered
great service, during the war of 1812, in assisting the women
and children in taking care of the harvests during the general
call, as harvest came on during the men's absence. I believe
all the white men in the township at that time, except, perhaps,
three, had to go. Miskel was a very large, stout man, and
worked almost night and day in securing the crops of his
neighbors. He lived to be very old. He did not know his own
age.

Benning Wentworth, father of Mrs. Finley, and grandfather
of Hon. I. J. Finley, served five years in the war of the Revolution as drummer, and three years in the French war; was a
native of the State of Maine. He emigrated to Ohio in 1816,
served for many years as justice of the peace, and was, I believe, the second male school-teacher in the township, a Mr.
Gilfillen being the first. School was taught in a log cabin, with
puncheon floor and oiled paper for glass lights. Phebe, his
wife, was the first female teacher in the township. All the
schools in those early days were sustained by subscription. Mrs.
Wentworth organized, I believe, the first Sabbath-school, which
she taught for several years at her own house. Mr. Wentworth
and wife were members of the Baptist Church. They lived to
a good old age, and died lamented and beloved by all.

A. P. Wentworth, the eldest son of Benning and Phebe
Wentworth, was an early settler, and lived in the township for
many years. He served during a long period as justice of the
peace, clerk of township, etc. Was still living in Kansas, at
last accounts, and holding office. Benjamin Wentworth, another
son, was one of the first in the township who kept a store. He
served for several years as justice of the peace, etc.; now dead.

Names of Pioneers and Incidents furnished by Mrs. Mary Hester.

James Finley, the father of Mrs. Hester, emigrated from Ireland in 1811; his family consisted of himself, his wife, and seven children—five sons and two daughters; John, father of Hon. I. J. Finley, and for many years justice of the peace, and who held other township offices, died in 1858; James; Moses, for many years township treasurer; William, served through the Mexican war, and died several years since of cholera in Cincinnati; Isaac, carpenter by trade, now dead; daughters, Mary (Mrs. Hester) and Jane. They traveled from New Haven to Pittsburg, over the Alleghany mountains, in wagons; from there they came in a boat to Manchester, and lived near West Union, on the banks of Brush creek, for a short time, when the country was little more than a wilderness, the nearest neighbor being three miles away. They came to Huntington township soon after. Seth Vanmeter, a noted backwoodsman and hunter, killed a large panther a short distance from his residence; it measured nine feet from tip to tip. It was not an unusual thing to scare up a bear in those early days, or to see droves of wild turkeys crossing your path, or herds of deer galloping over the hills, or to hear the wolves howling around at night. Snakes were very numerous. Mrs. Hester killed a large rattlesnake as it was passing through the cabin door; it had sixteen rattles on its tail.

Benjamin Rolston, the noted hunter, while out on his farm one morning saw quite a large bear, which he and his dogs attacked. The bear fought until she put the dogs to flight, when Rolston dispatched her with his gun. Mr. Rolston, while out one very cold night, lost his way and perished near his own home. Thus died one of the bravest hunters of his time.

Mrs. Hester is now living near the old Indian trail leading from Chillicothe to Portsmouth. Reuben Elliott emigrated from Virginia at a very early day; was a soldier in the Revolutionary war; died at the age of ninety, and was buried with the honors of war. Robert McCann was a soldier in the Revolution; fought under General Washington at Brandywine; kept hotel

in early days—sign, Three Kegs. Peter Clark, emigrated to
Ohio from Kentucky; he was slightly deranged, and was a great
hunter; would often fire the woods in large circles, for the purpose of shooting deer and other wild animals. Benjamin Malone emigrated to Ohio from Kentucky about the year 1800;
was bearer of dispatches from Chillicothe to Detroit after Hull's
surrender; he passed through Columbus before there was a
house erected in the place; is still living. William Heness emigrated to Ohio from Virginia; was a member of an independent company in the war of 1812, and took an active part in
the defense of Fort Stephenson. David Ogden served three
years in the war of 1812. James Gladstone emigrated from
Scotland at a very early day; traveled in a wagon from New
York to Pittsburg with his wife; floated down the Ohio river
in a canoe to Portsmouth; they traveled from Portsmouth to
Chillicothe on foot; settled in Huntington township when quite
a wilderness. James Wilson came from Kentucky to Ohio;
enlisted for the war of 1812 at the age of fifteen years; he is a
cooper by trade, and is still living. Stacey Devinney, millwright by trade; fought as a soldier in the battle of New Orleans, under General Jackson; was a great admirer of the old
hero. At the time Jackson was elected president in 1828, Huntington township gave him but eleven votes, I believe. At this
election John H. Robinson, or better known as "Hoopole" Robinson, made a bet of a barrel of whisky with Devinney that he
(Jackson) would not get that many votes, Devinney winning
the bet, of course.

Aaron Vanscoy's Reminiscences.

Mr. Aaron Vanscoy emigrated from Virginia to Ohio, in
1804, with his father, Aaron, Sr., in wagons; they settled in
Gallia county, and remained there five or six years; from there
they came to Ross County, and settled in Huntington township.
He was in the war of 1812, under Captain Northup, Colonel
Safford, and General Ed. Tupper; served six months; he belonged to a rifle company, and traveled on foot to Urbana; he

never received any pay, although promised six dollars a month; he furnished his own arms, clothing, blankets, etc. He has often, when the mud and water were knee deep, made his bed by cutting a pile of brush, and spreading his blanket on top of it. He afterward received a warrant for one hundred and sixty acres of land, which was all the compensation he ever had for his services. He is still living, at the age of eighty-two. He has seen hundreds of Indians in the early days in the township; he was a hunter, and has killed many deer, and helped to kill several bears, wolves, turkeys, etc., which were very plentiful when he first settled in the township. He has heard the screams of the panther where he now lives, on what is called Indian creek. He used to trap a great many wolves on his farm in early days.

Enoch Vanscoy was in the employ of the government during the war of 1812, driving hogs; is still living. Wm. Haynes, Rev. Isaac Murphy, of the Baptist denomination, John Campbell, Jacob Day, Benjamin Smith, and David Ridgeway, were in the war of 1812.

Henry Neborgall's Reminiscences.

Mr. Neborgall's father emigrated to Ohio, in 1808, with his family, consisting of six children, to-wit: Jacob, John, Catherine, George, James, and Henry, my informant, who has been a resident of Huntington township fifty-three years. He has seen many deer, turkeys, wolves, etc. He says, one day, when quite a lad, he was sent out by his father to haul wood near the house, and while thus employed he saw a gang of large wolves after the sheep in the field, and tried to get the dog to attack them; but the dog seemed to be frightened and would not go near them. He then took a billet of wood and drove them off himself, and saved the sheep. At another time, Mr. Neborgall's wife heard the screaming of a child in the woods at no great distance, and ran to see what was the matter. Upon arriving in sight of the child, she found it to be a cousin of Mr. Neborgall, named Waggey, who had been sent on an errand to a neighbor's house, and, to her horror and surprise, she saw that five large wolves had attacked the poor little fellow. About the time Mrs. Neborgall arrived, a Mr. Peter Cockerell came to their aid, and they drove the wolves away, thus, in all probability, saving the lad's life. On another occasion, Mr. Neborgall and a Mr. Joseph Haynes started one night to Chillicothe, with their marketing, on horseback. After jogging along for some time, they heard what they supposed to be the voice of some one hallooing who had lost his way in the thick woods, which were very common in those days. They answered several times, and the sound came nearer and nearer. The travelers were soon satisfied that it was no human voice, but that of the panther. They put whip to their horses, the screams still following nearer and nearer, until they came to a clearing where another neighbor lived, on the Limestone road, when their unwelcome follower left them, for which they were very thankful. Mr. Neborgall says he was very well acquainted with William Hewitt, the hermit. Mr. Neborgall lived near him during his hermitage, and visited him often. Mr. Hewitt came from Virginia about the year 1808, I think. He first hunted awhile on the Big Kanawha, where he killed bears and deer, and sold their skins to the hands at the salt works on that river. He used the bear-skin for his bed, and had a shanty made from the bark of trees. When I first saw Hewitt, forty-five years ago, he occupied a shanty made of bark on Crooked creek, near Mr. Daniel Shotts', not far from Farmersville. He lived there during the summer, and when cold weather came on he removed to a log cabin which had been built and roofed, on the land near James Toops. The cabin had no doors or windows cut out, and was erected on sideling ground, one side being raised some distance from the ground; the hermit dug the earth away on this side for an entrance. Here he lived for about four years, employing his time mostly by hunting, and sustaining himself on the meat of the bear and deer. One Saturday evening, while returning to his cabin near the Pinnacle Knob, he killed a small deer of the "toehead" species, as he called it. He tied its legs

together, swung it around his neck, and started on his way.
After going a short distance he saw a very large buck, and, as
he expressed himself, he "blazed away," and killed him. He
tied this one's legs together, as before, and thus, with his two
deer swung around his neck, he marched home. From this
cabin he removed to the celebrated cave on the Portsmouth
pike. Mr. Neborgall says he often visited him at his cave, and
he, in return, would visit at Mr. Neborgall's house, and was very
sociable after once becoming acquainted. He told me, says
Mr. Neborgall, that he came from Virginia, and told me often
the cause of his leaving and living as he did, not in just these
words, but gave me to understand the cause to be this: He was
married, and one morning he started on a tramp from which he
did not expect to return for several days; but from some cause
he returned that night, and on arriving at his home he found,
to his surprise, another man occupying his couch with his wife.
His first thought was to kill them both, but on further reflec-
tion concluded he could live alone, and enjoy himself in the
wilds of the forest, so he left for Ohio. He never returned to
Virginia, but used often to speak of his wife. His mode of preparing his vension was to take the fleshy parts of the hams,
and then build a fire of wood and let it burn to coals; he would
then drive sticks in the ground around the bed of coals, and
place thereon the flesh thus taken from the bones, letting it dry
very hard. This he would use for bread; the bony pieces he
would broil on the coals for his meat. He was a very large
and muscular man, and seemingly intelligent. His clothing
consisted of skins dressed by himself, which gave him the appearance of a wild man. He had in his cave his Bible, which
he read during the greater portion of the Sabbath day. He was
never known to hunt on that day. Mr. Neborgall says the last
talk he had with Hewitt was a short time before he became sick
so as to be confined to bed. He had quite a bad cough, and
said he had gone down on the Scioto bottoms for some purpose,
and was belated and overtaken by a very severe rain-storm;
it growing very dark he concluded he could not find his way,

so he built a fire in the forks of a large fallen hickory tree in the pasture of Mr. James Davis, and there awaited the return of morning. It rained on him all night, from which exposure he took a cold that finally put an end to this truly singular man. The following incident is related of him: A gentleman quite well dressed rode up to the front of his cave one morning, and without ceremony saluted him in this manner: "Well, old fellow, I have come to get the history of your life." Hewitt replied : "You leave here quick, or I will give you a history of hell." He left.

Mrs. Mary Hester, who was personally acquainted with Mr. Hewitt for several years, says he was a large, portly man, rather good looking, dressed in buckskin of his own make; he carried a long flint-lock rifle and a tomahawk, and depended on his rifle for subsistence. He would sometimes exchange his venison for salt and ammunition. He was an extraordinary singer and whistler. He occupied a small cave situated on the Portsmouth pike. There is a small mound erected to his memory above the cave. He was taken sick in his cave, but did not die there, being removed to Waverly before his death, where he was kindly cared for until he breathed his last. He was a peaceable, inoffensive man, of temperate habits, and generally beloved by all who were acquainted with him.

The cave is under a shelving rock which juts out about fifteen feet in the center, and extends fifteen feet each way from the center, and is about five feet high in front of the cave. The rocks have been torn away to some extent in constructing the Chillicothe and Portsmouth pike, which passes immediately in front of the cave. Under this shelving rock is another one, which was used by the hermit to build his couch upon. The cave is partly inclosed by a circular wall. The following is the inscription on his monument, erected by T. S. Hammon :

> WM. HEWITT, THE HERMIT, occupied this cave fourteen years, while all was a wilderness around him. He died in 1834, aged seventy years.

William Chestnut, Sr.'s, Reminiscences.

Mr. Chestnut emigrated to the Northwestern Territory in 1798, with his father's family, consisting of five children, to-wit: Daniel, William, Margaret, Polly, and Benjamin. Daniel Chestnut was in the Whisky Insurrection under General Washington. His grandfather emigrated from Scotland, and his grandmother from Ireland to Portsmouth, Ohio; from there they came on foot by the old Indian trail to what is now Chillicothe, and settled. They lived there four years, and then moved on the hill where they lived three years. He afterward purchased two hundred and sixty acres of land from General Massie on Indian creek, in Huntington township. The first abode of Mr. Chestnut was an old waste house, where he lived ten days. The bed was made of crotches and clapboards. The second dwelling-place, a tent made from an old wagon-cover. The cabin he built on the land he purchased from General Massie was sixteen by eighteen feet, and seven feet high, puncheon floor, old-fashioned style. Their food consisted of wild meat, such as bear, deer, turkey, etc., and hominy. The hominy was made in a wooden mortar or hand-mill. Every one would have to await his turn at this mill. Mr. Chestnut was a great hunter; he has killed all kinds of wild game. He had started to Chillicothe with his team at one time, and when on the way he met a very large bear, and concluded he was too good a prize to be lost. He took out his lead-horse and gave chase, carrying his rifle with him, and ran the bear some distance into the woods, where he succeeded in shooting him, after which he dressed and weighed him, finding that he made four hundred pounds net meat, perhaps the largest bear ever killed in Ohio. The meat was equally divided between himself and a neighbor, Wm. Thompson, and salted down. Wolves were very numerous in those days. Farmers who were lucky enough to have sheep had to build high pens for their protection. During one night Mr. Chestnut lost forty head of his best sheep by those sneaking rascals. The bears would frequently kill their hogs and carry them off into the dense forests. Snakes were also very numerous. Mr. Chestnut was once bitten by a copperhead, which confined him to his bed for several weeks. He served as the first justice of the peace for a term of seventeen years. Here I will give an incident that occurred in those early days, during his official term: A Mr. Ogden was in Chillicothe one day on some business, in company with a man calling himself Shears, who, in conversation with Mr. Ogden, told him that he wished to purchase a small piece of land in the vicinity of Chillicothe. Ogden told him he would sell him a piece, when Shears proposed to go home with him and look at the land. They started, Shears, having no horse, trudging along on foot. Getting late, Ogden proposed that his companion should get up and ride behind him, which proposition was thankfully accepted. It seems that Mr. Ogden had some money tied up in the corner of his handkerchief. All money in those days was gold and silver, and could not be so handily carried as we do our greenbacks in pocket-books now. Ogden had twelve or fifteen dollars in his handkerchief, and had put it in his coat-pocket, but did not think of such a thing as his friend behind him abstracting it. They traveled home together, and when they entered the cabin Mr. Ogden's children came fondling around him. After being seated, he felt for his money, and found that handkerchief and all was gone. Mr. Ogden went to Esquire Chestnut's, procured a warrant, and had Shears arrested, when he confessed the crime and gave up the money. The 'Squire ordered him to be committed to jail. Shears told the constable, after they had started on their way, he would rather take thirty lashes than go to jail. The night being very dark, the constable concluded that was the easiest way to get relieved of his prisoner and consented. Mr. Chestnut was directed to cut the switches; whereupon he went to the woods near by, and soon returned with five stout switches or withes. They then tied the prisoner to a mulberry tree near by, and Mr. Ogden commenced to apply them lustily to the prisoner's back. He would hit him a few cuts and then bathe his back with whisky, and exhort the prisoner to better deeds. After applying the thirty lashes, save one, the prisoner was untied and permitted to go his way, if not a better man, perhaps wiser.

Mr. Chestnut was captain of the militia for several years, and died April 23, 1851, aged eighty-three years. He helped to cut out the old Zane trace, now the Limestone road. He and a Mr. William Richie were chosen, and acted as spies to watch the movements of the Indians in the upper end of the county, while Colonel Barnes was stationed at Waverly with his men. The Colonel wished to get some orders from Chillicothe, and started on his horse, and the two spies on their mission on foot. When on the dividing ridge, a large turkey ran across their path. Richie threw off his blanket and gave chase. Barnes, in the meantime, coming up, saw the blanket lying in the path, and, supposing there were Indians about, wheeled his horse, and started back full tilt, when Chestnut, who was standing under a tree, sheltering himself from the rain—it raining hard—hailed him, and explained matters, when each went his way.

William Chestnut, at the breaking out of the war of 1812, volunteered the 9th day of May, 1813, in Captain William Rutley's company, under Colonel Denny, which was in General Tupper's brigade, and on the 10th of the same month started for Fort Meigs, and served about ninety days, when he returned to Chillicothe, and was there dismissed. He received a land warrant in 1824, and was paid eight dollars per month for his services. When a boy, Mr. Chestnut, in July, 1798, saw an Indian chief, Captain Johnny, shoot the war-chief Toa-willa-wa. The bullet entered his forehead, and scattered his brains for some distance around on the ground. His squaw was present at the time, and bemoaned her loss by tearing her hair and other demonstrations of her terrible sorrow. The chief was buried in his costume and armor. In 1798, an Indian, who was intoxicated, rode his horse round in a circle for some time. A white man by the name of Thompson was standing near, when the Indian exclaimed: "I killed Thompson's father and brothers," at which Thompson became so enraged he made for the Indian, and dealt him a heavy blow upon the head, which felled him dead at his feet. This so enraged the Indians of the neighborhood that they demanded Thompson, that they might avenge their supposed wrongs. But Thompson managed to escape, and fled the country. The Indians hunted for him for two long years, but Thompson did not return for seventeen years. Mr. Chestnut has been married twice. His last wife died October 24, 1869. He still lives on his farm with his grandson, Josiah Chestnut.

The following names of old pioneer settlers are furnished by Mr. Chestnut: Benjamin Chestnut, son of Daniel Chestnut, lives on his farm; was two years old when his father landed in Ohio. Lemuel Chestnut, carpenter, died at the age of sixty-seven. James Chestnut is living, and occupies the old homestead. John Chestnut was a farmer; is now dead. Peter Cockerell is still living, but very frail; aged eighty years; William Lockwood, now dead; William Selby, Sen., still living, and Larkin Selby; were all soldiers in the war of 1812. John Thompson was a great Indian killer in 1798. Hocery McAllister was in the war of 1812. Charles Chestnut was a famous hunter. Michael Thomas, whose name appears in another part of this work, was in the war of 1812, and in Wayne's campaign was one of the bravest men during the war, with Captain Keys, William Chandler, and Solomon Trego. Henry Montgomery emigrated to Ohio in 1797, and was drowned in Paint creek in 1800. George Funk was in the war of 1812; also, Francis Kile, Henry Strong, Lewis Wheaton, and Uriah Hurley.

Old Resident Settlers.

John Long, who served in the war of 1812, now dead, lived to a good old age. He held in his lifetime several township offices, and was beloved and respected by all who knew him. John Edgington lived in the township for many years; a good citizen; now dead. John Toops, shoemaker, is still living, and is very old. A. P. Riley, local preacher, is still living. Noah Hollis, still living, held several township offices. Jacob Bishop, blacksmith and carpenter, held several township offices; now dead. Daniel Shotts, quite a home hunter in his younger days, is still living. John Mendenhall, an old citizen, is still living. Henry Haynes is still living. Michael T. Streevey, an old hunter, has killed as many deer and wild turkeys, in his day, as any man of his age in the township; still living. William Thomas, a great hunter and fisherman, is still living. Jacob Sheets, tailor and farmer, is still living. John Gibson was a great singer and a good citizen. Benjamin Henis, now quite frail, has held several township offices. Jacob Blessing is still living, but very poor in health. Moses Finley, for many years township treasurer, has gone West. Richard Boyer, for many years justice of the peace and trustee of township. Andrew McCollister, for many years justice of the peace, school teacher, etc., moved West some years ago; is still living. Robert Ralston, a great raiser of stock, etc., is still living. His father, whose name appears in another place in this work, was a great hunter. Richard and Robert Elliott are still living. Ebenezer Rozell, Sen., I believe, was in the war of 1812; dead for many years. Milbourn Palmer held several township offices; now dead. Enos Rinehart, grocer, and trustee of township for several years, is still living. Henry R. Bishop, trustee of township for several years, is now living, but has been confined to his bed for several years with rheumatism. T. C. Robinson, still living, has served as township officer. David Nelson, still living, has held several township offices. John Scelig held several township offices; was captain of militia, etc.; is still living. P. G. Selby held township offices; is still living. Samuel P. Long, trustee of township for several years, is now keeping a hotel in Chillicothe. John Murphy is still living. B. S. Ruley, carpenter and farmer, for several years justice of the peace, trustee, etc., is living. John Clutz, farmer, is living. George Lytle, for many years constable, is yet living. John M. Haynes held several township offices; living. James Toops, trustee of township for sev-

eral years, is living. Abram Streevey served several years
as trustee of township; living. Bartholomew Reible, a resident for many years, is now in Minnesota. He emigrated at
an early day from Germany, and was truly one of our best
German citizens. Lawrence Lowery, farmer, emigrated to Ohio
from Germany several years since; living. James Lenox, Sen.,
emigrated from Ireland; was several years a resident of Huntington township; is quite aged; yet living. James Lenox, Jr.,
served several years as township trustee; is living. Benning
Wentworth, carpenter, a great marksman, hunter, and wrest-
ler in boyhood, is now living near Lattaville. Samuel R.
Posey, farmer, a Pennsylvanian by birth, served as trustee of
township. Francis Hester, German by birth, has been a resident of the township for several years, a good citizen; is still
living. Daniel Recob has been dead for several years. David
Miller, constable for several years, is now dead. Jacob Van
Gundy was constable for several years. Larken Selby was in
the war of 1812; dead for several years. Simon Johnson, was
drummer for militia during the war of 1812; still living.
Henry Cramer was in the war of 1812; is still living. Also,
John and William Miller. Hector Sanford emigrated to Ohio, in
1797, from the District of Columbia, in a canoe, with his slave
Thomas Watson. They landed at the big bend on the Scioto,
above the mouth of Paint creek. His entire record will be
given in full in another place. John England and Robert
McCollister, and another whose name is not known, voted in
the township for Andrew Jackson for President in 1824, he only
receiving three votes in the township.

David Shotts, father of Mrs. Margaret Bishop, emigrated to
Ohio from Virginia in the year 1810; was in the Revolutionary
war, and stood guard at Frederick city; was also in the Whisky
insurrection. He died, in the year 1825, in the following manner:
He had been away from home and was returning, when he was
overtaken, near his own home, by a severe thunder storm, and
took shelter under a large oak tree, which was struck by lightning; he was there found dead; there were seven other trees

struck near the spot, from appearances, at the same time. Mr.
Shotts was quite a hunter, and in early days killed several
bears, some two or three on his own farm. His family consisted of ten children, to-wit: Catherine, Jacob, Elizabeth, Margaret, Hannah, Mary, Daniel, Sophia, Susan, and Jonas, all
living except Catherine.

Jacob Grubb was in the war of 1812. He came to his death,
several years since, in the following manner: He and some two
or three neighbors went into Paint creek to bathe, Grubb
being a great swimmer. They were in the water sometime,
when, as Grubb was swimming across a deep hole, he was seen
to sink, and before he could be rescued was drowned. It is supposed he was taken with cramp.

George Ruffner emigrated to the Scioto Valley, in 1798, from
Kanawha, Virginia, and settled on the waters of Paint creek,
near Chillicothe. The foundation of his cabin is yet visible.
He was a fearless, brave, and daring hunter; had a great antip-
athy to the Indians, in consequence of the killing of his father
and mother by them, in 1791, on the Kanawha. He lived by
hunting panthers, bears, wolves, and deer, and would kill,
during his hunting excursions, any straggling Indians that
crossed his path. During the wars of 1791 and 1812 he served
as a spy. He moved his headquarters on the head waters of
the Mohiccan, was frequently in company with the renowned
Indian killers, Wetzel and Hughes. A few days after the
burning of Greentown, a party of Indians was discovered upon
the banks of the Mohiccan Lake. The discoverer was Bunty
Billy. It appears that the Indians had recognized Billy at the
same time he saw them. Billy at first attempted to run away,
but the Indians called to him to stop, telling him that they
would not hurt him; he stopped. The Indians approached
him in a friendly manner, calling him good boy, etc. "Do
you know a family by the name of Seymore?" asked a tall
Indian. "Yeth thir, I geth I do, thir," said Billy. "Do you
know a man by the name of Ruffner?" "Yeth thir, but I'd
thay to you, thir, not to put yourthelf in hith way, thir. He ith

a perfect devil, thir, when he ith not in a good humor, thir."
"All right," said the Indian, and the Indians took their leave,
and Billy hastened home to inform Ruffner of his discovery.
Instantly Ruffner seized his rifle and set out in pursuit of the
Indians. He soon got on their trail and followed them to the
cabin of Seymore. The Indians had entered the cabin door
when they were soon joined by Ruffner. On their entry they
appeared friendly, shaking hands with the whole family; nor
were the family alarmed, as the visitations of Indians were fre-
quent. But Ruffner's sudden appearance aroused the suspicions
of Philip Seymore. Ruffner thinking that they would not dare
to attempt an assault upon the family in his presence, insisted
upon Philip, as he was the most fleet on foot, to run into the
settlement and gather up some friends. As soon as Philip had
left the cabin, Ruffner immediately noticed a sudden change in
the countenances of the savages; they cast upon each other
significant looks and glances, as much as to say: "He is gone
for aid, and now is our time." A deep, death-like silence
now reigned in the lonely forest cabin. Kate Seymore could
no longer endure this deathly gloom. Advancing toward
Ruffner, she said: "Oh, Ruffner, we shall all be killed!" Ruffner, who had sat eyeing the savages with a tiger's look, sprang
to his feet and exclaimed, in a stentorian voice: "Imps of hell,
leave this place this moment, or I will send your bloody red
spirits to the burning pit of hell," advancing toward them.
Instantly the Indians sprang from their seats, and made an
attack upon the heroic Ruffner with uplifted tomahawks.
In the bloody conflict he killed three of the murderous savages,
but, being overpowered by their united strength, fell a lifeless
bleeding corpse upon the cabin floor. The remaining savages
then turned upon the aged and helpless couple, who sat like
petrified statues, gazing with a vacant stare upon the terribly
bloody scene around them. Two tall savages, with tomahawks
uplifted, dripping with the blood of the murdered Ruffner,
dealt each a blow upon their heads, and they, too, fell in the
agonies of death.

Poor Kate was an eye-witness to the dreadful tragedy. She was compelled to hand over all the money of her murdered father, and cook dinner for the murderous Indians. Immediately after dinner Kanotchey, the brutal chief, approached Kate and sunk his tomahawk deep in her head. She, too, fell to rise no more.

The savages then left the cabin, concealing themselves in the deep, dark forest. Philip, on returning with help, entered the yard, and seeing the bloody, mangled body of Ruffner, sprang into the cabin, where his worst fears were realized. The sight was shocking. Poor Kate, the once romping, laughing, beautiful, rosy-cheeked Kate—there she lay beautiful in death. Philip, on beholding her lifeless form, and those of his beloved parents and the noble Ruffner, gave vent to a flood of tears, and exclaimed: "'Tis done; I am left alone." Said he to his neighbors: "Blood for blood shall be my motto." Bidding them farewell, he bounded into the deep forest, becoming an Indian killer. His home was the forest; his covering, the blue sky; his food, wild meat. He would lay in ambush, and every straggling Indian that hove in sight he would kill. Near the close of the war, while seated on a high bluff near the Mohiccan, in a narrow bottom below, he saw a large, straight, tall Indian in shooting distance. He cocked his gun, took aim, fired, and killed the savage. He descended and walked to the place where the Indian lay. On examination of his costume and person, he found it was Kanotchey, the murderer of his sister. Philip said: "I am now avenged." He then returned to his home on the Mohiccan.

Race for Life, etc.

Michael Thomas, whose name appears in another part of this work, was a spy under Wayne, and traveled all over the Northwestern Territory. At one time, when out reconnoitering, he saw five or six Indians not far from him, and nearly at the same time the Indians saw Thomas and gave chase. Thomas, being very swift of foot, eluded his pursuers for some time, but the Indians could outwind him, and commenced gaining on him so fast he began to look for a hiding-place. As he ran along almost out of breath, he saw a large poplar tree which had fallen, and the bark from the log had fallen off and rolled up, and Thomas ran to it, threw in his gun and crawled in after. The Indians being so near, Thomas was almost sure they saw him, but it seems they did not. They came up and stood on the bark, immediately over Thomas' body, and he was sure they could hear his heart throbbing; for he says he thought it seemed to raise the bark above him with the Indians standing upon it. But to his astonishment and great satisfaction, the Indians passed on without discovering him. He lay in his hiding-place all that day, and when night came on he crawled from it and made his way to the first post of safety.

At another time when Mr. Thomas was out on a scout, while standing on the banks of the Ohio river, he saw coming down the bank, on the opposite side, three large Indians. He then hid himself. The Indians came down to the water and lay down to drink, when Thomas leveled his long and trusty rifle at one of their heads and fired, when the Indian tumbled head first into the turbid stream. The remaining two Indians fled into the deep forests, leaving their companion food for the fishes.

The Mistaken Shot.

Mr. Thomas and Peter Streevey, son-in-law of Thomas, and whose name appears in another part of this work, started out one fine morning on a bear hunt. After being out several hours, near where the Baptist church now stands, on the side of a hill, Thomas told Streevey he saw a bear at the foot of the hill through the vines and brush, and pointed out the object to Streevey. Streevey told him he did not think it was a bear, but Thomas insisted it was a bear, and told Streevey to shoot. Streevey refused, saying it was no bear, but if he thought it was to shoot it himself. But Thomas still insisted on Streevey's shooting, when he finally consented and fired. When the would-be bear fell, they heard the jingle of a bell, and Thomas exclaimed:

"You rascal, you have shot my breeding mare;" and when the two hunters reached the spot, behold, to their astonishment there lay Thomas' old black mare, stone dead. In those early days the horses and cattle of the pioneers were allowed to range at large, and would travel for miles away among the hills and valleys, and the owners would put bells on their stock, so that they could be more easily found when needed.

Natural Curiosities, etc.

The Alum cliffs are on Paint creek. What is called the court house is a circular formed cave, the circle being about three hundred feet around, the rocks projecting over about twenty or thirty feet, from which the water trickles down continually. At the north end of this circular cave is a solid rock twenty feet square. The cliff of rock is about four hundred yards in length, and about one thousand feet above the level of the water, with alum and other salts. There are several other caves, one about thirty feet in hight, and extending into the rocks considerable distance. Another cave is called the bake oven, by the old pioneers, from its similar appearance. All the way around the cliff is a ledge or layer of rock about four feet apart; the under or lower layer is about four inches and the upper layer about two inches in thickness. On the other side of the creek is a similar layer of about the same thickness and like kind of rock. It seems as though at one time they were united, but by some eruption of nature had been sundered to make way between the hills for the passage of the stream. Also, at the north end of this circular cave, is another cliff, about half a mile in length, of solid rock. In this cliff is another circular cave about one hundred yards in circumference, and extends back under the rocks fifty feet, and about one hundred feet in hight. About one mile from this cave is still another large cliff about six hundred feet in hight and three hundred yards in length, which, from some unknown cause, took fire, proving thereby that this earth contains elements of its own destruction. This fire burned without cessation for the space of nine months. At the north end of this cliff are three ancient graves covered with stone, about three feet high and twelve feet in length. In these cliffs is a kind of mineral pronounced by a geologist to be sulphurous acid; there is also saltpeter to a considerable extent. Several years ago some gentlemen, whose names are forgotten, undertook to and did manufacture saltpeter there, but not finding it in quantities sufficient to pay, abandoned the undertaking. · The cliffs are situated on the banks of Paint creek, which name was derived from the Indians, there being a bank of red clay on said creek, near the beautiful village of Bainbridge, where the Indians, before going on their war path, would resort to paint themselves with this red clay. In early days these cliffs were a great harboring place for wild animals, such as panthers, bears, wolves, and foxes, and many an old hunter has been foiled in securing his game by its hiding in those rocks and caverns.

These cliffs, as seen from below, present one solid mass of jutting rocks, extending far out over the beholder's head in many places, and looking as though about to tumble down and crush him to atoms, which inspires him with astonishment and awe. The top of the cliff is crowned with spruce pines, which can be procured very handily, and the citizens of Chillicothe often resort thither to procure those evergreens to decorate their halls and ball rooms. Those who are fond of viewing natural curiosities would be well repaid for their trip. Indeed, I know of no place where there is such grand natural scenery. It is visited in the summer season by hundreds, and often has been a place of resort for pleasure; and many social parties have met on these rocky hights for the purpose of having picnics, etc. These cliffs are owned by the Hon. Ex-Senator William Allen, and are about six miles from Chillicothe. Our venerable friend, Mr. Robert Bishop, Sen., who lives near these cliffs, showed us several ancient curiosities picked up near them, which he has in his possession, such as stone axes, chisels, darts, and arrows of various sizes; petrified horns of different kinds, shapes and sizes; bee combs, wedges, land turtles; bark and roots; stones, supposed to have been

used by the aborigines for skinning their game; pipes, etc., of
different shapes and sizes. On Mr. Bishop's farm is a sulphur
spring and deer lick. Near the cemetery on Bishop's hill, at
the head of a branch, is a graded fall of about one hundred feet.
And on the farm of Mr. George Long is a beautiful and pictur-
esque fall, almost perpendicular, of twenty or thirty feet.

Ancient Works.

About four miles southeast of the village of Bourneville, on
what is called Black run, a branch of Paint creek, are two quite
curious fortifications. The first, a stone wall, incloses about
one acre of ground; the wall is three or four feet high and
forms almost a square, with inner walls, forming partitions as
it were; the walls have been much higher from appearances.
The second works are situated about two hundred yards south,
and are thrown up in a perfect circle, with stone, about six feet
high and three hundred feet in circumference; nearly half of the
wall has been washed away by the creek. On the inside of this
circle, and in the center, is quite a mound thrown up of stone,
which is nearly one thousand feet in circumference, and is eight
or ten feet in hight, with a large white walnut growing immediately on the top.

Near Mr. Aaron Vanscoy's, on Indian creek, at the head of a
branch, is quite a mound of stone near where an old Indian
trail used to pass; the mound is several feet in hight. There
is a story connected with this mound which says: Several
years ago some brave young men concluded they would explore
the mound and ascertain what was buried within it. They
went to work and commenced to tear away the stones. After
they had worked some time, all at once it commenced blowing, thundering, and lightning at a tremendous rate, when
they became frightened and ran for their lives.

On Mr. John Dunn's farm, on Paint creek, is an ancient work
thrown up in a circular form; the distance around this circle is
about three hundred yards, and about four feet high. On Mrs.
Houlse's farm, adjoining, is an Indian mound some ten or
twelve feet in hight, about sixty feet long and forty wide.

On the south side of Paint creek, near the Chillicothe and Huntington pike, and about five miles up the creek, near the old dam, is an old salt well, where a considerable amount of salt was made several years ago, but it is now abandoned. The well is on the lands owned by Mr. John Dunn, of Chillicothe; it was bored by General McArthur, I believe.

Indian Battle Grounds.

In 1790, a termination was put to the war, which, for several years, had raged between the Creek Indians and the State of Georgia. Pacific overtures were also made to the hostile tribes inhabiting the banks of the Scioto and the Wabash. This being rejected, an army of 1,400 men, commanded by General Harmar, was dispatched against them. Two battles were fought near Chillicothe, Ohio, on Paint creek, in the territory included in Huntington township, between successive detachments from this army and the Indians, in which the latter were victorious, cutting off almost the entire detachment.

Franklin Township.

The soil of Franklin is generally thin. With the exception of along the branches, as Stony creek, etc., the lands next to Chillicothe, along the Ohio canal, are reasonably good. One side of the township is bounded by this canal and the Scioto river. At this portion of the township, on the river, there is a large and beautiful bottom, which, for richness of soil, can not be surpassed by any lands in Ross county, or perhaps the State. It is owned principally by Messrs. Foster, Davis, and Higby. The first settlements in the township were made on the river. The other portions of the township were very little settled for several years afterward. The larger portion of this territory is very broken and hilly. There are no pikes in the towdship, and the roads are generally bad, the canal being the principal outlet for exporting their grain, cord wood, tan bark, etc. A good road along the bank of this canal is needed badly. The timber is principally oak of the different varieties.

Present Township Officers.

Justices of the Peace, Elias Schamehorn and Samuel Wood; Treasurer, J. C. Foster; Trustees, Wm. McGayer, T. C. Foster, and David Crockett; Clerk, C. D. Higby; Constables, James Dawson and Jacob Piles. Post-office Alma.

John Foster's Reminiscences.

Colonel Foster's father came to Ohio in the year 1796, on an exploring expedition. He first went to Kentucky to see his brother-in-law, whose name was Cheneworth. He came up the Ohio river to the mouth of the Scioto, and up the Scioto in a canoe. In 1798 he emigrated with his family to Ohio from Cumberland county, Md. He first settled in Ross county, now Pike. From there he removed to the farm (where Colonel Foster is now living) on the banks of the Scioto, and lived in a log cabin about one year, and then built a hewed log house, the first house of the kind erected in the township. It is now standing and in good condition. Mr. Thomas Foster's family consisted of eight children, six daughters and two sons, John and Joseph. The latter died in the State of Indiana, in 1864 or 1865, at the age of seventy years. John was born August 4, 1801. He has lived in the township all his life, and occupies now the room in which he was born. He is now nearly seventy years of age, but his well-preserved physical condition would not indicate he had reached that period in life. He is a practical farmer, and one of the representative men of that great interest. His father had five brothers, Thomas, John, Benjamin, Joseph, and Richard. Richard was the first settler of Franklin township, when all was a dense wilderness, filled with wild animals of all kinds. Colonel Foster has held several offices during his lifetime, both civil and military. He represented the county in the legislature in 1848; was associate judge for a short time, when he resigned; was colonel of militia for several years, and held township offices, etc., for many years. His family consists of nine children, all living, to-wit: Joseph, William R., Mary Davis, Thomas, Jane Davis, John W., James P., Samuel D., major in late rebellion, and Rebecca Ann.

Rev. John Foster, of the M. E. Church, uncle of Colonel Foster, was born in 1771, died in 1839, was in the war of 1812 as captain of a company, and was father of twelve children, to-wit: Sarah, Ruth, Catherine, Betsy, Joseph, John, Casandra, Mary, Rachel, Thomas, Rebecca, and Nancy. Lewis Foster, another uncle, was born December 26, 1760, and died at the age of ninety-two or three. Colonel Foster's father and his father were the first white men who rowed the canoe up the Scioto river. A Mr. Cheneworth came to Ohio the summer before Mr. Foster, but they came in wagons. T. C. Foster, son of Colonel Foster, has seven children, to-wit: Martha, Hannah, James, John, William, and George. James served from August, 1861, to January, 1866, in the late rebellion, in the

33d, 53d, and 59th Ohio Volunteers, and some months in an
Illinois regiment the last year of the rebellion, and six months
on Veatch's staff; was major of regiment eighteen months;
was at the battle of Shiloh, siege of Corinth, battle of Corinth,
and in Sturgis' defeat and battle of Tallulah, and is now treasurer of the township. Colonel Foster has forty-five grand-
children and two great-grandchildren.

List of Old Settlers — By Colonel Foster.

John Johnston was justice of the peace for twenty-three
years; James Greearly, first school teacher; Quin Collins
Goddard; Samuel Wilson built first mill; Richard Tomlinson,
hotel-keeper at Three Locks or State dam, was justice for several
years, captain of militia, auctioneer, etc.; John and George
Pushon were in the war of 1812; William Ridenger; Enos
Moore; John Beauman; Elias Scammehorn, justice of the
peace for many years; Joseph Crockett, one of the first settlers
on Stony creek; Jonathan Swyers; Daniel Swyers was a Revolutionary soldier and was at the battle of Lundy's Lane; Allen
Nixon; Thomas Louzatta; Saul Phillips; Benjamin Phillips;
J. E. Higby, extensive farmer on the river, and father-in-law
of Hon. J. H. Keith, of Chillicothe; Sylvester Higby, a justice
of the peace for several years, held other township offices;
Samuel Wood held township offices, was justice of the peace,
etc.; Peter Bennett held township offices, and was captain of
militia; S. O. Barker, justice of the peace for many years,
township clerk, etc.; James Pry; Edward Hurdell. Joseph
Hern emigrated to Ohio from Germany in 1817; Mr. Hern
was a soldier under Bonaparte, and was at Strasburg when
Bonaparte was driven back from Russia. He went as a substitute for his brother, who is now drawing a yearly pen-
sion for his services, which Mr. Hern seems to think un-
just. He will be seventy years old in April next, and is
hale and hearty, and looks as though he might live that much
longer; he is a farmer, and keeps also a grocery store on the
banks of the Ohio canal. Just below Mr. Hern's grocery are

the three locks and the State dam across the Scioto river. The dam is nearly one hundred yards in length, and is quite a resort for fishing parties, and Mr. Hern is always prepared to entertain guests on those occasions in the best style, with anything they may call for. Thomas Tomlinson was the first lock tender, and Richard Tomlinson was the first grocer, at these locks.

Mr. James Davis' Reminiscenses.

His father emigrated to Ohio in 1808, and settled on the high banks of the Scioto. His family consisted of eight children, to-wit: William, Lotha, James, Hannah, Mary, George, Charles, and Louisa. They removed to Franklin township about 1815. He has held township offices in different capacities almost all his life. He used to be a flatboatman, and take his boats to Natchez and New Orleans trading. This occupation he followed for many years. He would sell his cargo and boats, and then foot it home. James has held different township offices. On his father's farm there was an old Indian burying ground, containing at first about twenty acres, which has from time to time been diminished by the washing away of the bank by the river, and is now almost extinct. They used to find many human bones, beads, etc., near and on the ground occupied by this graveyard. There are on the farm some four or five ancient works of different shapes and sizes, and some of them of considerable extent. There is also on this farm a salt spring or deer lick. On James Davis' farm, some years since, a company bored an oil well some seven hundred feet in depth; but, like many other companies, they failed to strike *ile.* At the mouth of Stony creek, General McArthur, several years since, bored a salt well, and made a considerable quantity of salt of a very good quality, but it was finally abandoned. On Mr. Davis' farm is what is known as the Foster Chapel, erected forty years since, and is a good substantial building yet. It belongs to the M. E. denomination. Mr. Davis' family consists of three children, to-wit: Emma, Mary E., and J. Russell Davis.

In earlier days, Franklin was a great place for game, such as deer, bears, panthers, wild cats, etc. Indians, when Mr. Foster first settled on the river, were very plenty, and they had a trail passing along up the Scioto, which was perceptible for many years. About two miles from Mr. James Davis' farm is a circular-formed basin, some ten to twenty feet deep, which has the appearance of having at some time been much deeper. This basin is about fifty to sixty feet across, and must have been dug out for some purpose by the aborigines many years since.

We have been shown by Mr. J. C. Foster a beautiful robe, made of four deer skins, which he himself had captured in the hills of Franklin. He is quite a hunter, and says that there are some of those beautiful and timid animals to be found in the neighboring hills yet, which almost tempted us to try our hand. We were shown by Mrs. James Foster quite a large and ancient split-bottom chair, which measured across the seat two feet and nine inches, and was used by her grandmother in her lifetime. The old lady was a very large woman, weighing about four hundred pounds; was born November 13, 1770, and died in the spring of 1841, aged seventy-one years.

Twin Township.

Officers of Township.

Justices of the Peace, Allen Cochran and Thomas Platter; Trustees, David Moore, Benjamin Poole, and Robert P. Mc-Cracken; Treasurer, J. Holter; Clerk, Abram Sommers; Constables, James Hanawalt and Jacob Roberts; Land Appraiser, William A. Jones.

Old Settlers.

W. A. Shoults' father, John Shoults, emigrated to Ohio from Rockingham county, Virginia, in 1812; was in the war of 1812; was a blacksmith, wagon and cabinet-maker; died aged eighty-two years and six months; lived on Paint creek forty years. His brother, Christian Shoults, emigrated to Ohio at the same time, and died some years since in the State of Indiana.

Jacob Shotts was born in Augusta county, Virginia; served as county commissioner one term; was trustee of township for several years; has lived on Paint creek for forty-six years. David Shotts, son of Jacob, served several years as trustee of township; was captain of militia. Joseph, another son, served several years as justice of the peace.

Ancient Burying Ground.

On Mr. Higby's farm, adjoining Mr. Shotts' lands, is quite an extensive ancient burying ground, where many human skeletons have been found; some of them of very large size. On the farm of Mr. A. Roberts, there is another burying ground. Last summer, the hogs rooted out of the earth the entire frame of a man of very large size. The under jaw bones would easily go over an ordinary man's face.

Old Settlers.

Hugh Cochran emigrated to Ohio from near Lexington, Kentucky, in the year 1797; was in the war of 1812; served during the war, and died aged seventy-five years. His sister, Elizabeth, was the first woman married in the Scioto Valley. In Howe's History of Ohio, we find the following account of the same: "On the 17th day of April, 1798, the families of Colonel Worthington and Dr. Tiffin arrived—at which time the first marriage in the Scioto Valley was celebrated, the parties being George Kilgore and Elizabeth Cochran. The ponies of the attendants of the wedding were hitched to the trees along the streets, which were then not cleared out, nearly the whole town being a wilderness."

James Browning's father, Joseph Browning, was a soldier in the war of 1812; was a tailor; died aged sixty-five years.

John Lance's father emigrated to Ohio from Pennsylvania in 1808; was a weaver; died aged sixty-eight years. John, now living, aged sixty-seven years, is a harness-maker.

Daniel P. March's father, Stephen March, emigrated to Ohio, from the then Territory of Maine, in the year 1817; was judge of the court and justice of the peace for many years; died aged sixty-five years. His brothers, Henry and Joseph H. March, were in the war of 1812. Joseph served a part of the time as a substitute for a hotel-keeper living in Kentucky, who was drafted. His wife's distress, in regard to losing her husband from home, moved the sympathies of Mr. March, and he offered himself as a substitute and was accepted.

Isaac Conner emigrated to Ohio from New Jersey in the year 1805, and was in the Revolutionary war; died aged eighty-two years. His son, John C. Conner, of Bourneville, served in the war of 1812, in Captain David Sutton's company, for six months, and was paid, after he was discharged, at the rate of eight dollars per month, and received a land warrant for one hundred and sixty acres of land also. He furnished his own uniform, consisting of linsey pants and home-made linen shirts.

They rendezvoused at Newark for about two months; from there he went to Urbana; stayed a short time; then to Finley's blockhouse; from there to Sowlon's town; remained a short time; from there through the Black swamp to the rapids of the Maumee; where he remained a few days, when part of the brigade was ordered back to Fort Meigs, where they were discharged. His company suffered terribly by exposure to the cold and wet; they had to wade rivers, swamps, etc.; had often to cut brush and pile them up so as to make themselves a place to lie upon to keep their bodies out of the water and mud. They made their bread by mixing flour with water; then, wrapping the dough around sticks, held it to the fire to bake. He says they were often put on picket guard at eight o'clock in the morning, and not relieved until the same hour next morning, and sometimes it was raining and freezing all night. His brother, Joseph Conner, who died from exposure while in the service, was only eighteen years of age, and of a delicate constitution; he was buried with the honors of war. J. C. Conner is a millwright and surveyor; has served as township officer for many years in different capacities; was treasurer fifteen years, and was captain of militia. He further says, at one time during his soldier life, there was one morning one hundred men sent out to stand picket guard, and they were kept out until the next morning at eight o'clock—the night being very severe, raining and freezing all the time—and out of the one hundred men, only nineteen lived. Among the number who died was his brother above mentioned.

Gideon Coover, father of John Coover, emigrated to Ohio from Pennsylvania, in the year 1800; was drafted to serve in the war of 1812, but furnished substitute; died aged forty-seven years. Samuel Coover emigrated to Ohio in 1808; was a tailor; died aged eighty-eight years. David Coover, brother of Samuel, died aged seventy years. William Campbell emigrated to Ohio at an early day; he was a resident of Twin township for sixty-five years; served during the war of 1812, and was one of the bravest soldiers in his regiment. John

Campbell, his son, a farmer, is still living. Thomas McDonald emigrated to Ohio, from Scotland, at an early day; served in the war of 1812; now dead. David Somers emigrated from Virginia at an early day; was a soldier in the war of 1812; now dead.

Shredrich Wroten emigrated from Delaware in 1806; was a soldier in the Revolutionary war; served five years and six months; was sergeant in his company; died aged eighty-nine years and six months. His son, Laban Wroten, has served his township for several years as constable and captain of militia; was a grocer and farmer; as a home hunter, has killed many bears, deer, turkeys, wild cats, etc.; had been, in his younger days, quite a muscular man, and in early times when corn huskings, log rollings, raisings, etc., were in vogue, has had many a hard fought battle, in the way of fisticuffs, and it was but seldom that he did not come off victorious. John Freshour, Sen., emigrated to Ohio, from Virginia, at quite an early day; he was one of the first settlers on Paint creek; was a soldier in the Revolutionary war; died aged eighty-five years. One of his sons, Daniel Freshour, was in the war of 1812; is still living. John, another son, died aged seventy-one years; was quite an extensive farmer on Paint creek. James McMillen, carpenter, now dead.

Simon Johnston, Sen., was one among the earliest settlers; was a soldier in the Revolutionary war. Barney Minney was in the war of 1812, and died while in the service. Job Harness was in the war of 1812; John Harness also; is now dead. Thomas Dehart, miller, was in the war of 1812; now dead. Nelson Prather, farmer, dead. Enos Prather was quite an extensive farmer on Paint creek in his day; he removed to Kansas several years since, where he lately died.

Ralph Chaney, father of James Chaney, was an early settler; has been dead for many years. He came to his death in the following manner: He was out one day felling a tree, and the wind, blowing very hard, threw it the way he did not expect it to fall, and caught him under it.

Allen Cochran, Sen., father of John and Allen Cochran, Jr., served as justice of the peace, in Twin township, for fifteen years; died aged sixty-two years. Isaac N. McCracken was justice of the peace and associate judge for several years. David Cochran, one of the early settlers, furnished wood for the legislature at its first sitting in Chillicothe.

Richard Acton emigrated to Ohio, from Kentucky, in the year 1800; was a soldier in the war of 1812, under Major Willett; died aged forty-five years. His son, Jacob Acton, of Bourneville, harness-maker, has been a resident of Twin township thirty years; he was two years and seven months in the service of the United States, as a sailor on the Levant, a first-class sloop of war of twenty-six guns—six of them Paxton guns of eighty-four pounds; two fifteen pounds; the balance thirty-two pounds. John Hannawalt, tailor, emigrated from Pennsylvania to Ohio, in 1820; lived in the village of Bourneville over forty years; served as captain of the Independent Riflemen at one time; is still living; aged seventy-two years.

The village of Bourneville contains about one hundred and fifty inhabitants, two stores, three groceries, one saloon, three churches, three blacksmith shops, one tannery, two harness shops, two shoemakers, two wagon-makers, one post-office (postmaster, Abram Sommers), one cabinet-maker, one carpenter's shop and cabinet-maker's combined.

In this village, in the month of October, 1844, there was a brutal murder committed. Frederick Edwards was a storekeeper at the time, and, being a bachelor, he slept in the store, and was reported to have a considerable amount of money. Two fiends in human shape, by the names of Thomas and Maxwell, concocted a plan for robbing Mr. Edwards; and breaking into the store for that purpose—not expecting to find any one there—they were attacked by Mr. Edwards, and a terrible struggle ensued, in which the latter lost his life. Thomas and Maxwell made their escape, but were afterward captured, tried, and found guilty. Thomas was hung in Chillicothe, in March, 1846. Maxwell made his escape, aided, as some suppose, by a woman from Cincinnati, who claimed to be his wife, and was never recaptured.

John McNeal, father of Robert McNeal, was a resident of Twin township for over fifty years; died aged seventy-five years. His son, Archibald, was a soldier in the war of 1812; died aged sixty-five years.

Abijah Flora, a carpenter, emigrated from Virginia to Ohio, or the then Northwestern Territory, at a very early day; he served in the war of the Revolution as lieutenant of his company; was one of the first settlers in Heller's bottom, on Paint creek; died aged seventy years. His son, Thomas, has been a resident of Ross county upward of sixty years; he was called out during the war of 1812, and furnished a substitute. He was a great hunter in his younger days; and when quite a lad he went on a hunting expedition with his father and the Rev. James B. Finley, William Murphy, Jacob Myers, and Simon Girty, Jr., son of the noted Simon Girty, of historical notoriety. The company started with dogs and guns, and upon arriving at a small creek—now known as Black run, the dividing line between Huntington and Twin townships—on the farm now owned by Mr. John Schligle, of Chillicothe, just above the barn now being built on the left of the road, the dogs treed a bear up a large poplar, of which tree the stump and part of the body still remain. They managed to shoot the old bear, and cutting down the tree found two young cubs. Mr. Flora says he enjoyed the sport finely, and would like to live those days over again. At another time, his father and Mr. George Vincent Heller were out walking one Sunday morning, through the beautiful forest bottoms of Paint creek, when they discovered some bear tracks in the soft ground, and followed them to a large elm tree, and found there was a den in the hollow of the tree several feet up. They started to inform their neighbors, and soon collected quite a number of men, women, and children, who with dogs and guns went along to see the fun. The first thing they did was to cut a small tree and lodge it against the one containing the bear; this accomplished, Mr. Jacob Heller went up the tree which had been lodged, and found the hole in the tree extended several feet down in the body, but they managed to get Mr. Heller a long papaw pole, to which they attached a bunch of hickory bark, which they set on fire, and, when in full blaze, Mr. Heller thrust it down in the hollow of the tree. Bruin soon made his appearance at the entrance of the hole, when George Heller raised his gun to shoot; he told Jacob his head was in the way; he answered to fire away, as he was the matter of an inch or so out of the way; his brother fired, and the fur from the bear flew into his face and eyes, so close was he to the bear. The bear fell to the ground, and, amidst the howls of dogs, and shouts of men, and screams of women and children, bruin was hastily dispatched.

At another time, a Mr. Murphy treed a bear, and collected several of his neighbors, with their dogs and guns; among them Mr. Flora, my informant, then quite a lad. The tree was hollow, and when it fell the tree broke in two where the hole was. An old bear and two cubs rolled out, and immediately took to flight, the dogs and men in full chase; they soon overtook and dispatched them

On returning, they passed by the tree which they had felled, when Mr. Flora, out of curiosity, stooped down and peeped into the hollow tree as it lay, when, to his surprise, out jumped another yearling bear, which took after him. He ran a short distance, and, finding the bear about to overtake him, he turned and ran back, the bear in full chase. He mounted the stump of the fallen tree, when the dogs came to his relief, and soon one of the party of men came up and dispatched the bear with his rifle, much to the relief of the boy.

Names of Old Settlers.

The first preacher was William Kerns, and the first school teacher a Mr. Wilcox. William Reed was justice of the peace for many years. John Core and James Russell served in the war of 1812; Benjamin Brackey, Presley Johnston, John Reed, and David Breedlove emigrated to Ohio, from Kentucky, in early days. Peter Shanks, Alex. Johnston, Thomas Ladd, George Kilgore, Philip Maston, Robert McMahon, and Daniel Devoss were among the first settlers in Heller's bottom, on Paint creek. When they first settled there they owned a fine young sow, with a brood of pigs, which they had to fasten under their cabin at night, to prevent the bears from carrying off. Late one night they heard the squealing of their sow, and knew a bear had made his way to her by some means, and was carrying her off into the forest. They hastily arose, all in their night clothes; the old lady prepared a torch by splitting a clapboard or two, and Mr. Devoss called several neighbors from their cabins near by, and they with their dogs and guns gave chase, the old lady carrying the torch and lighting the way. The dogs soon overtook the bear with his burden, and the men coming up, dispatched bruin, and rescued the sow but little injured; but the men and old lady, in running through the nettles, which at that time were very thick and waist high, had their naked legs terribly pricked and scratched. Mr. Flora says when a bear captures a hog, he does not stop to kill it, but will hug it in his arms and commence eating until he has finished his repast, the hog squealing all the time as long as life lasts.

George J. Moore emigrated to Ohio from Pennsylvania in 1813; was a farmer; died in 1850. His son, David Moore, lives on the Milford and Chillicothe turnpike. In constructing said pike, several human skeletons were dug up near his house, some of them of very large size and some very small, as though of infants. Also, on Mr. Philip A. Road's farm, others, of similar sizes, were found.

Daniel R. Dolohan says his father, Michael Dolohan, emigrated to Ohio from Virginia about the year 1802; was in the service in the war of 1812, as scout; died aged ninety-one years. Thomas Hanks emigrated to Ohio about 1790; was a soldier in the Revolutionary war; his sons, Joseph and John, were soldiers in the war of 1812; all dead. David Collins and a Mr. Miller built what are known as the Slate mills, on the north fork of Paint creek, which was one of the first flouring mills in the county. Jesse Wiley, Casper C. Pliley's father, Philip C. Pliley, William Pliley, and Jefferson Pliley emigrated to Ohio at a very early day. Their father was in the Revolutionary war. John Ward died in Hardin county, in 1867, at a very advanced age ; was in the war of 1812, under General Harrison.

Benning Wentworth gives us the names of James Matthews, who emigrated from Scotland to Ohio in early days, and was treasurer of Highland county for a term of years, and Robert Waddle, also from Scotland, who was under Wellington at the battle of Waterloo, and a great player on the bag-pipe.

Peter Shaner emigrated to Ohio from Pennsylvania in 1800 ; served in the war of 1812, and helped cut out the Lebanon road, and is now living, aged eighty-six years. His father, Peter Shaner, Sen., was in the war of the Revolution, fought at the battle of Brandywine, and died at the age of seventy. John Gossard emigrated to Ohio from Pennsylvania, in 1808 ; was in the war of 1812, and served several years, in different capacities, as township officer ; died aged fifty-six years. Philip Gossard and Jacob Gossard served in the war of 1812 ; are now dead. James Nichols, miller and hotel keeper at the Slate mills in early days, served in the war of 1812 ; is now dead. Henry Sharp served in the war of 1812, and as justice of the peace for many years. Dilard Rowe, Abott Rowe, and David Rowe served in the war of 1812. Charles Craig and John Craig were in the war of 1812, and their grandfather was in the Revolutionary war. Alex. Craig and a Mr. Wilson were the first school teachers for many years. William Craig was the first man who drove a wagon and team to Chillicothe over Zane's trace.

Colonel John McDonald.—(*From the Scioto Gazette.*)

" Colonel John McDonald was born January 28, 1775, in Pennsylvania. His early life was spent upon the frontiers of Pennsylvania, Virginia, and Kentucky. Before arriving at the age of twenty years he entered the military service, under

General Wayne. He was attached to the army commanded by that veteran general in 1794, and was present, on the 20th of August of that year, at the memorable battle with the Indians on the Maumee. In 1796 he came to Chillicothe, where he was married to Miss Catherine Cutwright in 1799. He settled on Poplar ridge in the year 1802. He held, in his lifetime, various offices in the militia, and served as colonel. In the war of 1812 he went with the Ohio troops to the frontier, in the double capacity of paymaster and quartermaster, and was taken prisoner at the surrender of Detroit. In 1813 he was appointed a captain in the regular army. In 1814 he was placed in command of a regiment of regular troops at Detroit, and remained in the service until peace was made and the army disbanded. In 1817 he was elected to the Ohio senate, and served for two terms. At a late period of his life he wrote and published a very interesting and popular work, comprising sketches of the first settlements on the Ohio, with biographical sketches of distinguished pioneers. Colonel McDonald was very extensively known, and greatly respected as an intelligent and useful citizen ; and so long as the early history of the Scioto Valley shall be preserved, he will be kept in honorable recollection."

Rev. James B. Finley gives the following account of Colonel McDonald [See Finley's Autobiography, pp. 123–130] :

" Colonel John McDonald, one of my early companions, was of Scotch descent. His father was connected with the army of the Revolution from its first organization up to the year 1780. John was born in Northumberland county, on the 28th of January, 1775. His father crossed the mountains with his family in 1780, and settled at a place called Mingo Bottom, three miles below the present site of Steubenville. The Ohio river was then the extreme frontier, constituting the dividing line between the white and red man. No line, however, was sufficient to form a barrier against the invasions of both parties. The white man was as frequently the aggressor as the Indian, and many were the scenes of suffering, carnage, and massacre witnessed along this border line. My young friend was reared

amid all the dangers of a border war.   In the year 1789 his
father removed to Washington, Ky., where we were then resid-
ing, and soon after their arrival my acquaintance with young
McDonald commenced.

"The first excursion of my friend McDonald was taken
with Kenton.   Three men from near Washington went out on
a hunting expedition, and encamped on the waters of Bracken,
about ten miles from home.   While they were out hunting a
party of Indians came upon their camp, and placed themselves
in ambush, to waylay the hunters on their return at night.
The names of two of the hunters were Dan Figgans and Josiah
Wood ; the name of the other is forgotten.   It was late when
the party returned.   As they were preparing their supper the
Indians crept up stealthily, and fired, killing Wood and the one
whose name is forgotton.   Figgans, being unhurt, fled for his life.
The Indians started in pursuit, with the most hideous yells.
The race was most fearfully kept up, but Figgans distanced his
pursuers, and at midnight reached Washington, where he
alarmed his friends at Kenton's Station.   This bold warrior
immediately mounted his horse, and, in a short time, having
raised a company, started in pursuit.   Young McDonald was
anxious to accompany them, but his father, thinking him too
young, being but fifteen years of age, to be of any service,
refused his consent.   He was not, however, to be deterred ; so
stealing his father's rifle and horse, he started at full speed, and
soon overtook the company.   They arrived at the place about
sunrise, and a most shocking scene presented itself to their
view.   One of the men had been scalped, and thrown into the
fire, where he was nearly consumed ; the other had also been
scalped, and cut to pieces with the Indian hatchet.   The party
proceeded to the mournful work of depositing their remains in
the ground ; and ascertaining by the tracks of the horses that
the Indians had directed their course for the Ohio river, they
started after them.   When they arrived at the river, they found
that the Indians, without waiting a moment, had plunged in
and swam across, thus cutting off pursuit.   This dreadful sight

had a tendency somewhat to cool the ardor of the youthful warrior, who, nevertheless, would have been glad of an opportunity
for taking revenge upon the savage foe.

"From this time McDonald was constantly engaged with
scouting, hunting, and surveying parties. In the spring of
1792 he joined General Massie's settlement at Manchester,
twelve miles above Maysville. This was the third settlement
on the northwest side of the Ohio river, above Cincinnati, or
Losantiville, as the town was called. This infant settlement,
together with the lives of all in the station, was in constant
danger. Many and exciting were the scenes by which they
were surrounded. Sometimes they were deeply depressed, and
anon, when danger was over, their spirits rose exulting at the
trials and conflicts through which they had passed. A report
would sometimes come in that one of their number had fallen
by the hand of the enemy, which would cast a shade of sadness
and gloom on all hearts; then again the intelligence that the
bold and daring hunter had captured the foe, would inspire
them with courage. Thus life was made up of constant alterna-
tions of hope and despondency. This constant warfare made
the early settlers so familiar with scenes of blood and carnage,
that they became, in a measure, indifferent spectators, and at
the same time reckless and fearless of all danger. Scenes of
horror that would have congealed the blood in the veins of
those unaccustomed to them, would scarcely move the heart of
the hardy pioneer.

"In the spring of 1794 Colonel McDonald and his brother
Thomas joined General Wayne's army, as rangers, or spies.
The company of rangers consisted of seventy-two, of whom
Captain Ephraim Kibby was commander. He was a true Jersey blue, fully adequate to any emergency growing out of his
highly responsible position. It was the duty of the rangers to
traverse the Indian country in every direction, in advance of
the army. This was not only a toilsome, but a dangerous work.
The company was divided into small detachments, which

started out in every direction, and, after scouring the country, returned and made their report to headquarters.

"Early in November of the year above mentioned, Mr. Lucas Sullivan, a land-speculator and surveyor from Virginia, collected a company of twenty-one men to go upon a surveying tour into the Scioto country. This was a hazardous undertaking. Notwithstanding the Indians had been severely beaten by General Wayne, a few months previously, yet the country was far from a state of peace. Attached to this company were three surveyors, namely, John and Nathaniel Beasley, and Sullivan, who was the chief. Young McDonald was connected with this company. Every man carried his own baggage and arms, consisting of a rifle, tomahawk, and scalping-knife. While engaged in surveying, the hunters would go in advance as spies, and the surveyor, chain-carriers, and marksmen would follow in line, the whole being brought up by the pack-horse and the man who cooked for the company. It was his business to keep a good look-out, so that the enemy should not attack them in the rear. In this military manner was most of the surveying in Ohio and Kentucky performed. They did not carry any provisions with them, but depended on their rifles for a living, which seldom failed to afford them an abundant supply.

"Having taken Todd's trace, they pursued their journey till they came to Paint creek, at the old crossings. From thence they proceeded to old Chillicothe, now Frankfort, and thus on to Deer creek, where they encamped at the mouth of Hay run. In the morning Sullivan, McDonald, and Murray went down to Deer creek with the intention of taking its meanderings back to the camp. They had not proceeded more than a hundred rods till a flock of turkeys came flying toward them. McDonald and Murray being on the bank of the creek, near to a pile of drift-wood, Murray, without reflecting a moment that the turkeys must have been driven toward them by some persons, slipped up to a tree and shot a turkey. He then slipped back, and as there were more turkeys on the tree, McDonald slipped up to the position left by his companion. Just as he was about to fire, the sharp crack of a rifle fell on his ears, and, turning instantly, he saw poor Murray fall to rise no more. Looking in the direction from whence the messenger of death came, he saw several Indians with their rifles leveled at him. Quick as thought he sprang over the bank into the creek, and they fired but missed him. The Indians followed hard after him, yelling and screaming like fiends. Running across the bottom, he met Sullivan and three others of the company. Sullivan instantly threw away his compass and clung to his rifle. Their only safety was in rapid flight, as the Indians were too numerous to encounter. As they ran the Indians fired upon them, one of the balls striking Colvin's cue at the tie, which shocked him so much that he thought himself mortally wounded. But he was a brave young man, and being fleet of foot, he ran up the creek and gave the alarm at the camp, stating that he believed all were killed but himself. Those at camp of course fled as soon as possible. McDonald and his party ran across the bottom to the high land, and after running three miles struck a prairie. Casting their eye over it, they saw four Indians trotting along the trace. They thought of running round the prairie and heading them, but not knowing how soon those in pursuit would be upon them, and perchance they would get between two fires, they adopted the better part of valor and concealed themselves in the grass till the Indians were out of sight. After remaining there for some time they went to the camp and found it deserted. Just as they were about to leave, one of the company espied a note stuck in the end of a split stick, to this effect, " If you should come, follow the trail." It was then sundown, and they knew they would not be able to follow the trail after dark. When night came on, they steered their course by starlight.

" They had traveled a distance of eight or nine miles. It was a cold, dreary night, and the leaves being frozen, the sound of their footsteps could be heard some distance. All at once they heard something break and run as if it were a gang of buffaloes. At this they halted and remained silent for some time. After a while the fugitives could be heard coming back softly. Supposing that it might be their companions, McDonald and McCormick concluded to creep up slowly and see. They advanced till they could hear them cracking hazel-nuts with their teeth. They also heard them whisper to one another, but could not tell whether they were Indians or white men. They cautiously returned to Sullivan, and the company, after deliberation, finally concluded to call, which they did, and found, to their joy, that it was their own friends who fled from them. They had mutual rejoicings at meeting again, but poor Murray was left a prey to the Indians and wolves. They now commenced their journey homeward, and, after three days' travel, arrived at Manchester."

Names of Old Settlers, furnished by Col. John C. McDonald, Jr.
Alex. Given emigrated to Ohio from Pennsylvania about 1800; was in the war of 1812; bought land of General McArthur and paid for it by months' work; died of cancer in 1858. Isaac Pearce. Aaron Foster emigrated from Pennsylvania to Ohio; was in the war of 1812; was adjutant under Colonel John McDonald; served as justice of the peace for twenty-one years; was county commissioner one term; died in 1862. Samuel Teter emigrated to Ohio from Washington county, Pennsylvania, about the year 1798; had four sons, Samuel, George, John, and Daniel; all served in the war of 1812, except Samuel; all dead. John Core emigrated from Maryland to Ohio in 1800; was a millwright and blacksmith, and built the first mill in Twin township; his three sons, John, Henry, and Chrisley, served in the war of 1812; Chrisley started the day after he became eighteen years of age. Henry was sergeant-major on Colonel McDonald's staff during the war. William Reed emigrated from Delaware to Ohio in 1798; was justice of the peace for several years. Philip and Daniel Hare emigrated from Delaware in the year 1797; Daniel was captain of a company during the war of 1812, under Colonel McDonald. David Elliott was captain of a company in the war of 1812. Benjamin

Turner emigrated from Delaware to Ohio at an early day. Samuel Turner was one of the first hotel-keepers. Nathan Reeves and Ephraim Camper were the first school teachers. Jacob Myers served as major in the war of 1812; was one of the bravest officers of his regiment; he was a carpenter. John Mahan was in the war of 1812. John Walker built one of the first mills in the township; was a blacksmith. John Summerville emigrated from Scotland to America, and settled in Twin township at an early day; was quartermaster under Colonel McDonald during the campaign of 1814; served as justice of the peace for many years; is still living. James Summerville was in the war of 1812, and was killed in the battle of Tippecanoe. Archy McDonald emigrated to Ohio from Scotland. He came as a British soldier, but deserted and joined the American forces; was at the surrender of Lord Cornwallis. His two sons, John and William, served in the war of 1812. Joseph and Jacob Myers were in the war of 1812. Colonel John C. McDonald, Jr., who furnishes the above, is living, aged fifty-nine years, but his well preserved physical condition would not indicate that he had reached that period in life. He is a practical farmer, and one of the representative men of that great interest. He served one term as sheriff of the county, to the credit of himself and county, and refused any further honors in that line, although his many friends would have been pleased to have given him their suffrages. He served during his time as land appraiser, and filled several township offices.

Reminiscences by James P. Brown.

"I was born in Fauquier county, Virginia, and emigrated to Ohio in 1816. Lived several years on the south branch of the Potomac, in Virginia. Was a volunteer in the war of 1812, under one Captain Ashby; was at the battle of Hampton Roads, under Generals Cobin and Crutchfield; the latter ordered about six hundred of us to advance and fire on about two thousand of the enemy. After giving the order, Crutchfield ran, and was not seen by his men until they found him about twelve miles distant from the fight. There were seven or eight of our men killed. We stood the fire of the enemy for some time, until it became too hot for us, and then retreated. General Cobin was wounded in the wrist. The ball went up his arm and came out at the elbow. He was on one side of a post and rail fence at the time he received the wound, and the enemy all around him, when one of our men broke down the fence and took him to the rear with his horse. Just before receiving his wound, he called to Captain Ashby, saying: 'I know you and your men will fight; fight on!' But he was soon wounded, and ordered a retreat. One of our men, John Barr, was shot through the leg, and cried out: 'Oh, Lord, I am dead!' I took his gun to carry, when Barr got up and took to his heels, soon passing me in his flight; he had only received a flesh wound. After the fight was over, we commenced preparing our repast, which was composed of spoiled provisions, cooked in a few old rusty kettles." My informant says he paid two dollars and fifty cents per week for his board, and rations thrown in; he was not paid off for some time after being discharged, and had to pay his own way home. He is now living, aged eighty-three years. His father, Daniel Brown, was of English descent, and was a a distiller in Virginia. He settled in that State during the war of the Revolution, and had eight sons and eight daughters.

John Camelin, father of Mrs. John Baum, emigrated from Pennsylvania to Ohio about 1800. Was called out during the war of 1812, but furnished a substitute; died aged about ninety-one years. Was born on the fourth day of July, 1776, the day of the Declaration of Independence.

By James Demoss.

James Demoss, Sen., emigrated from Ireland at an early day; was a soldier in the war of 1812; was a painter; died during the war by disease contracted while in the service. Benjamin Grimes, one of the early emigrants, settled in Heller's Bottom at quite an early day, and was many years a class leader in the Methodist Church; was married four times; died several years since in Fayette county, Ohio. His son, George Grimes, is now living on what is known as the Barger farm, near the village of Bourneville. On Mr. Grimes' farm is quite an extensive circular fortification, containing about eight acres; the embankment is now some eight or ten feet in hight. Near Mr. Demoss' dwelling, a few years ago, while the hands were working the public road, in digging into a bank they found an entire human frame of a very large size. Old settlers, William McCauley, Matthias Cooney; physician, Isaac Verden.

By Mrs. McKenzie, mother-in-law of Mr. William Igo.

Her father, Daniel Hare, emigrated from Pennsylvania to Kentucky, and from there to Ohio, in 1796. Her husband's grandfather was a drum-major in the Revolutionary war, and served seven years. Her husband, Mr. McKenzie, was in the war of 1812, as captain of a company for some time, when the companies were consolidated, which relieved him; died aged about eighty years. He was for many years a leader in the M. E. Church. Mrs. McKenzie says her father came to Ohio without bringing his family, for the purpose of hunting and laying up a supply of meat for the next summer. He first chopped down a large tree, and cut it off some twelve or fifteen feet long; this he split in two and dug them out in the shape of troughs; the one half he filled with buffalo, bear, deer, and wild turkey, and salted them down; then placing the troughs together, one on top of the other, he covered it with a lot of brush so as to deceive the Indians, telling them that when he came out in the spring, and the brush had become dry, he intended to burn that log up. In the spring when Mr. Hare and his family arrived, they found their meat all right. At one time Mr. Hare went to watch a deer lick, and after fixing up a blind and being seated some time, he heard something approaching him through the brush in his rear, and upon turning around, near him, was a large panther crouching, and in the act of springing upon him; he fired his rifle at the panther, when it made one terrible scream and took off through the thick woods one way and Mr. Hare the other, fully satisfied to leave for the present.

Mrs. McKenzie is now aged about seventy-nine years; she and her mother were the first two white women who settled on Paint creek. Her playmates were the young squaws, and she says, "many a romp have I had with them, and as fearless of danger as though they had been white children." "When we first settled on Paint creek, father had to go to Limestone for our meal and salt; some times we would use the hominy block in lieu of going to the mill for meal." At one time when her father was away from home, some Indians came to their cabin and asked her mother for salt, they being very fond of that article. The old lady refused to give them any. One Indian became enraged, and said: "My gun shoot by and by." But the old lady did not give them the salt, and they left seemingly much enraged. She, after they had left, feared they would return before her husband and do some mischief. But they did not; and when he returned, she told him how the Indians had treated her in his absence, whereupon he went to the Indian camp and informed their chief that one of his men had been at his cabin and insulted his wife. The chief called up the guilty Indian, and snatching the hatchet from Mr. McKenzie's belt, he beat the Indian over the head with it at a terrible rate. The Indian cried piteously during the castigation, and when the chief returned Mr. McKenzie's hatchet, he told him that that Indian would not trouble his family any more, and he did not. Mrs. McKenzie says her father was a great hunter in his time, and killed many bears, deer, turkeys, panthers, buffalo, etc. The buffalo used to mix with their farm cattle and were quite tame. Her father first settled near the big falls of Paint creek, on General Massie's land, and while living there she has heard the screams of the panther and wolf in the night quite near their cabin. The first school teacher was David Reed; the first preachers were William and Edward Carnes; the first school house was built on the lands now owned by Howard Newman.

By William Igo.

His father, Lewis Igo, emigrated from Pennsylvania to Kentucky in the year 1794, and from Kentucky to Ohio in 1798, and bought the first land on Twin creek from General McArthur. It was the first tract of land sold by him in the county. My informant, born and raised on the same farm, and still living on it, is now sixty years of age. His father, on first arriving in the country, procured meat for his family by hunting in the dense forests of that then wilderness; and for meal, he made occasional trips to the mills in Kentucky, or manufactured it himself by a hand-mill. When they first settled, their nearest neighbor was at the Slate Mills, on the north fork of Paint creek, where R. R. Seymore now lives.

On Mr. Igo's farm is an old Indian trail, which leads from Pee Pee to Old Chillicothe. The trail in places is yet quite perceptible.

My informant's brother, Paul Igo, who now resides in the State of Illinois, was the first white child born in Twin township. He was born in February, 1799.

I was shown, by my informant, a powder-horn and pouch that has been in use in the family over one hundred years. The strap is made of elk skin, and the pouch of buckskin. Its first owner was a great hunter, and has carried it thousands of miles through Virginia, Kentucky, and Ohio.

Near the house, one night, Mr. Igo's father heard a disturbance among his sheep. He got up, and taking his loaded gun, went out to see what the trouble was, leaving his ammunition behind. He heard the dogs in full chase after something, which they soon treed on a large stump several feet high. Upon drawing near, he discovered an animal of some kind on the stump, and, taking as good an aim as the darkness would admit, fired at it. He then called to his wife to bring him some ammunition and the ramrod, which he had left at the house in his haste. His wife soon brought the ammunition, but forgot the ramrod. There was near the stump a lot of blue-ash chips, where Mr. Igo had been hewing some puncheons. They raked the chips together, and he set fire to them, telling his wife that, as he could go more quickly back to the cabin after the ramrod, she had better await his return. The old lady, being a little nervous, said she would not stay there, but go herself, which she did. By this time, Mr. Igo had quite a fire burning from his chip-pile, by the light of which he saw on the stump a large panther, his eyes glaring down upon his pursuer like two balls of fire. Mr. Igo soon reloaded his trusty rifle, and fired the second shot, which took effect in the head of the panther, but too low down to penetrate the brain. The animal now began descending the stump backward, while Mr. Igo quickly reloaded his gun, and when the panther neared the ground, he fired again, the ball passing through its body, soon putting an end to its life. It measured nine feet from tip to tip.

By Henry Pool.

J. W. Pool, the father of Henry, emigrated from Maryland in 1813. He left his native State on the day of Perry's victory on Lake Erie; lived in Ohio exactly ten years, and died at the age of fifty; he was a blacksmith. Henry Pool is now sixty-five years of age. His father-in-law, George Vincent Heller, and also Jacob Vincent Heller, were in the Indian fight on Paint creek, at the Reeves' crossing. George was one of the chain-carriers who assisted in laying out the city of Chillicothe.

Mrs. Henry Pool says that she lived in Heller's Bottom with her father for several years. She particularly remembers one winter. In February, a deep snow had fallen, and was followed by rain. Mr. Heller had several tenants on his land at the time, and among them one named Russell, who lived with his family in a small cabin. On the evening of the storm, Mr. Heller told the men they had better move out of their houses, as a flood was coming, and the bottom would be inun-

dated before morning.   Mr. Heller's house being on high
ground, they all moved to it with their families, except Russell, who sent his family out, but could not himself be per-
suaded to leave his cabin.   The water shortly began to rise,
and soon flooded the lower part of the house.   He then took a
kettle, filled it with coals of fire, and ascended to the loft of the
cabin.   But soon the water began to make its appearance there
also, when he commenced calling for help, but amid the roar-
ing of the flood it seems no one heard him.   He finally took a
cake of deer's tallow, which he found in the cabin loft, and,
taking off his shirt, tore it into strips, which he wrapped
around the tallow, and then set it on fire with the coals in his
kettle.   Tearing off a portion of the roof, and elevating his
light on a pole, he soon attracted the attention of his friends,
who came to his relief in a dug-out, and conveyed him to safe
ground.   In the morning his cabin could nowhere be found, the
flood having carried it away.   During the inundation, says
Mrs. Pool, one of the neighbors lost a fine two-year old heifer,
and one day, when hunting for her, after the water had sub-
sided, he found her hanging by the neck in the fork of a buck-
eye tree, fourteen feet from the ground, quite dead.   What
would our farmers, living in Paint creek valley, say if such a
flood should make its appearance in these days?

Mr. Heller was one of the first farmers who brought
sheep into the county.   He was a local preacher and justice
of the peace for many years.   On the farm of Joseph Ross,
some years since, stood a large hollow sycamore tree, with a
hole cut in one side in the shape of a wedge, wide at the top,
and cut down to a point, which is supposed to have been done
by the Indians for the purpose of catching wolves, by placing
meat on the inside so as to induce them to place their necks in
this notch.   Mr. Heller at one time started out to watch a deer
lick, on the land he owned on Paint creek.   After he had prepared his blind, and had been seated a short time, he saw a
large bear jump up on a large poplar log near the lick, and in
a few seconds a large panther made its appearance on the other

end of the log. They made for each other, and when they met
the bear struck the panther one powerful blow with his paw,
and knocked him off. Mr. Heller did not stay to see the fight
finished, but made a hasty exit for home. One day a Mr.
Daniel Devoss, whose name appears in another place, and who
lived on the ridge near what is called the Spruce hill, was out
hunting his horses, when he met a neighbor's boy hunting
cows, each having a dog with them. When passing along
near the northwest side of the hill, the dogs commenced a furious barking a short distance from them. When Mr. Devoss and
the lad approached near the spot, they saw a large panther,
who was jumping at their dogs from under some pine brush.
When they came up the panther made a spring down the hill,
the dogs following him, but they soon brought him to bay,
and by clubs and stones, and the assistance of their noble dogs,
quickly dispatched him. At another time Mr. Devoss was
hunting his stock, which had strayed into Huntington township, and on the farm formerly owned by Mr. Daniel Toops (an
old settler), but now the property of Nathan Ward, near where
the house now stands, he saw a large panther lying behind a
log, which instantly sprang up and ran a short distance, and
then stopped and looked at Mr. Devoss, who, having neither
dogs nor gun, quietly retired and left him to his own reflec-
tions.

Ancient Works.

Near Bourneville, and overlooking the beautiful valley of
Paint creek, with the pretty town of Bainbridge in the distance, is what is known as Spruce Hill, the name being derived
from the large amount of spruce pine growing thereon. The
crest of this hill, or mountain, is surrounded by a stone wall
five or six feet in hight in some places, and from appearances
has been much higher, but the hand of time has caused it to
sink and crumble down. This wall surrounds the entire crest
of the hill, or mountain, is almost circular in form, and is

nearly three miles around. On this hill, within the inclosure, are found cinders, or dross, as if caused from the melting of some metallic substance. At the base of the hill, Paint creek flows over a bed of solid slate rock, and at low water may be seen two or three round holes, or wells, neatly cut out in the rock, about the size of an ordinary well, with closely-fitting covers or lids over the top.

On Joseph Baum's farm, near Bourneville, is an earth fortification thrown up, which is now from three to four feet in hight, with outlets or gateways at each corner. The embankment, or wall, is formed in a perfect square, embracing about thirty acres. On the farm of George Baum, adjoining that of Joseph Baum, is quite a large mound, from three to four hundred feet in circumference at the base, perfectly round, and some thirty feet in hight. On the line between the lands of John Storm and Joseph Baum, is another fortification, in shape resembling the letter J, containing twenty-five or thirty acres.

Near the same place, on Mr. Baum's land, are three large pools, or basins, which were evidently scooped out by some race of people long since passed away. One of them is twenty or twenty-five feet in depth. There are large trees growing in these places, and near them are found pieces of broken earthenware in abundance, human bones, teeth, etc. On the same farm is another work, built of stone, the whole resembling in shape a horse shoe. On the lands of the Messrs. Cochran, numerous pieces of earthenware have been found in plowing every spring from many years past.

Buckskin Township.

Township Officers.

Justices of the Peace, John H. Carr, James Bell, and John Coder; Trustees, John Carr, Calvin Parrott, and John Murray; Treasurer, D. O. Diggs; Clerk, Steward Evans; Constable, William Davis; Notary Public, Henry Hester; Land Appraiser, John Parrott; Postmaster, Levi Pricer—Office, South Salem.

The village of South Salem contains about three hundred inhabitants, two stores, three blacksmith shops, two wagon shops, two carpenter shops, four churches (two Methodist, one Presbyterian, and one colored), one grist and saw mill, two school houses (one white and one colored), and one cemetery.

By Henry Hester.

His father emigrated to Ohio in 1804, from West Pennsylvania; was in the war of 1812 as a lieutenant of a company; served as clerk of the township for many years; was by trade a millwright; died aged fifty-two years, in Chillicothe. James Wilson. John H. Wilson served many years as justice of the peace in the township, and was in the war of 1812; now dead. John Morton emigrated from South Carolina in early days; now living. First preachers, Rev. James Dickey, who was pastor of the church in South Salem for twenty years; Hugh Fullerton was also a pastor for twenty years. Frederick Parrott was in the war of 1812. John Wallace served for many years as justice of the peace. Satterfield Scott served as county commissioner one term, and for many years as justice of the peace; now dead.

By Alexander McGinnis.

His father, James McGinnis, emigrated from Pennsylvania to Ohio in 1801; was in the war of 1812; was a shoemaker by trade; was also a home hunter of considerable notoriety; he killed many deer and other game; my informant says he would kill some days five or six deer, and hang them up in the woods, and then send him and his brother to bring them home; he died aged seventy-two years. His grandfather, James McGinnis, emigrated to Ohio at the same time; served in the Revolutionary war six years, and was wounded in the thigh with a ball which he carried to his grave; lived in the township about twenty-two years; was a shoemaker; died aged eighty years, and retained almost the vigor of youth to near his death. Alexander McGinnis is now sixty-nine years of age, and has lived in the township about sixty years; is a local preacher of the Methodist Church. He says the first house built in South Salem was by a Mr. Douglas, in 1846 or 1847, and he built the third one in the place. His wife's maiden name was Taylor; her father emigrated from New Jersey, in early days, to Ohio, and served in the war of 1812; was at Hull's surrender; he was an elder of the Presbyterian Church for forty years, and died aged eighty-two years. George Pricer, Michael Hare, Robert Edminston, Jacob Davis, Abram Dean, Robert McGinnis, Captain Nathan Kilgore, and Captain Daniel Hare, were all in the war of 1812.

How Buckskin Derived its Name.

Buckskin creek derived its name in the following manner: At the time of the settlement of the township, the Indians had a camp at Old Chillicothe (now Frankfort), and they made a raid among the white settlers, stole some horses, and committed other depredations along said creek. When the whites made a search for them, they found them camped near the creek on the land now owned by Daniel Cline, where stood a very hollow sycamore, which had a large opening in the side at the root.

In this hollow the Indians had hung their skins—mostly deer—and built a fire under them for the purpose of drying them. When the whites attacked them, the Indians fled, leaving their skins to the whites. This circumstance gave the name to Buckskin creek, and afterward to the township.

By Doctor Hamilton.

He emigrated from Pennsylvania to Ohio in 1839. He built the house in which he now resides, in South Salem, in 1847, and has practiced medicine in that vicinity ever since; was educated at Jefferson College, Pennsylvania, and attended the University of his native State. After moving to South Salem he was very instrumental in building up the village, and especially the Academy.

By Willis Graham.

His father, whose name was George, emigrated from the State of Maryland in 1804; served as a soldier in the war of 1812; was a carpenter and cabinet-maker; died aged eighty-four years and ten months.

By Joseph Vanderman.

His father, whose name was John, emigrated from Pennsylvania to Ohio in 1800; he and his brother Frederick were in the Revolutionary war, and took an active part in the battle of Brandywine; they served under General George Washington. John Vanderman was a tanner; was a great hunter, and depended upon his rifle for sustenance for himself and family for several years in the first settlement of the country. At one time the Indians stole a fine bay mare from him; he and a younger man gave chase, and trailed them for several miles, when they found themselves surrounded by the savages, but they boldly dashed through them and made their escape. He died aged eighty-six or seven years. Joseph Vanderman served at one time as lieutenant of a militia company; never held any other office, though often solicited. His brothers,

John, Matthias, Conrad, and Henry, were all in the war of 1812,
except Conrad, who died on his way to the army. He was a
finely educated young man, and died beloved by all who knew
him.

By Mrs. Frances Wilson.

Her husband, John H. Wilson, emigrated from Pennsylvania to Wheeling, Virginia, and thence to Kentucky. In 1800,
he came to Ohio. He was in the war of 1812; served as justice
of the peace for sometime; was a consistent member of the
Presbyterian Church for a great many years, and died at South
Salem in 1865, aged eighty-seven.

By John G. Caldwell.

His father, James Caldwell, emigrated to Ohio in 1805;
was sergeant of his company under Captain Kilgore, and served
his township for many years as justice of the peace and clerk,
etc.; he also taught school in different townships for several
years. His son has several books, in manuscript, written by
him, of a religious nature; he died aged sixty-three years.
The following statistics, taken from some of his old books, and
papers published in 1827, which had been preserved by his father,
may be interesting to our readers:

Associate Judges of Ross County in 1827, Isaac Cook,
James Armstrong, and Thomas Hicks; Clerk of Courts, Su-
preme and Common Pleas, Recorder and Clerk of the United
States District Court, Humphrey Fullerton; Sheriff, Thomas
Steel; Coroner, Josephus Collet; Commissioners, John Mc-
Clain, Wm. Wallace, and E. Fenimore; Notary Public, John
A. Fulton; Postmaster, William Creighton; Justices of the
Peace, Levi Belt, and Wm. Creighton, Sen.; Attorneys-at-law,
Wm. K. Bond, Joseph Sill, Platt Brush, Thos. Scott, Richard
Douglas, Wm. Creighton, Jr., Edward King, Henry Brush,
Samuel Treat, and Levi Belt; Physicians, John Edminston,
Joseph Scott, James Hayes, Samuel Monett, Jr., Samuel McAdow,

and William Heath; Merchants, John Carlisle (wholesale and retail), W. R. Southard, John Walker, T. V. & S. Swearengin, Barr & Campbell, Ephraim Doolittle, Wm. McFarland, Wm. Ross & Co., John McCoy, Nimrod Hutt, Waddle & Davison, Isaac Evans, John Hutt, James Culbertson & Co., Runkle & Beard, James Phillips, John McLandburgh, Amasa Delano, David Kinkead & Humphrey Fullerton, Thomas Orr, Marquis Huling, Waddle & Dunn, James McClintock, Wm. McDowell & Co., Samuel Taggart, James Miller & Co., John McDougal, Austin Buchanan, Wm. Irwin, Drayton M. Curtis, and Samuel Monett; Innkeepers, Edmund Bayse, Thomas Cohen, Daniel Madeira, James Phillips, and Benjamin Woods.

Town Council of Chillicothe in 1827.

Levi Belt, Mayor; Jeremiah McLean, Recorder; Benjamin Hough, Treasurer; Isaac Cook, W. R. Southard, John Waddle, James McDougal, David Kinkead, and George Nashee.

Bank of Chillicothe—Thomas James, President, and John Woodbridge, Cashier; Farmers', Mechanics', and Manufacturers' Bank of Chillicothe—Thomas S. Hyde, President; John P. Fessenden, Cashier.

The following lines are taken from a copy of the *Scioto Gazette* of 1815:

THE YEARS TO COME.

My transient hour, my little day,
Is speeding fast, how fast away;
Already hath my summer sun
Half its race of brightness run.
Ah me! I hear the wintry blast,
My "Life of Life" will soon be past;
The flush of youth will all be o'er,
The throb of joy will throb no more,
And fancy, mistress of my lyre,
Will cease to lend her sacred fire.
My trembling heart—prepare, prepare,
For skies of gloom, and thoughts of care;

Sorrows and wants will make thee weep
.And fears of age will o'er thee creep.
Health that smil'd in blooming pride;
Will cease to warm thy sluggish tide;
The shaft of pain, the point of woe,
Will bid the current cease to flow.
And who, alas, shall then be nigh
To soothe me with affection's sigh,
To press my feeble hand in theirs,
To plead for me in silent prayers,
And cheer me with those hopes that shed
Rapture o'er a dying bed.
Days of the future cease to roll,
Upon my wild, affrighted soul.
Mysterious fate, I will not look
Within thy dark eventful book;
Enough for me to feel and know,
That love and hope must shortly go;
That joy will vanish, fancy fly,
And death dissolve the closest tie.
E'en now, while moans my pensive rhyme
I list the warning voice of time;
And oh! this sigh, this start of fear,
Tells me the night will soon be here.

By Mrs. Matilda Hitchcock.

Her father, whose name was John Proud, emigrated to
Ohio from New Jersey in 1801; he served as a soldier in the
war of 1812; he was constable of his township for many years;
was a great hunter and paid for his farm, on which my informant, with her husband, now resides, in pelts and furs. He
bought his land from General McArthur. He first lived two
years on what was formerly known as the old Read farm, near
Bourneville, when he moved to Buckskin township, which,
at that time, was a howling wilderness, there being no settlement north within twenty miles. When he was moving to his
new home in the woods, he took his family and a part of his
goods to his cabin, and leaving them in care of his wife,

returned for the balance. By some cause he was delayed until the next day, leaving his family in their solitary cabin, which his wife had to defend all night, standing with the ax in her hands to keep the wolves out, as it had no door except what was very commonly substituted in those days, a blanket or quilt. He was a great hunter, and, at the age of seventy years, with spectacles on, he would kill squirrels from the tops of the highest forest trees with his rifle. He was a man of no education, but of a great mind—one of nature's true noblemen. He died at the age of seventy-four years.

By Samuel Braden.

His father, Robert Braden, emigrated from Pennsylvania in 1800. He was in the war of 1812, and lived in Buckskin township forty-two years, where he died at the age of seventy-one years. My informant has been a resident of the township for seventy years, and is now aged seventy-three years. Old settlers, David Edminston, Robert Edminston, Robert Holding, J. Wilson, Benjamin McCline, Michael Hare, Robert Young, Jacob Davis.

By C. W. Price.

The village of Lyndon, on Marietta and Cincinnati Railroad, contains two stores, a grocery, a blacksmith shop, a carpenter shop, a wagon shop, a hominy mill, a planing mill, a saw and flouring mill, town hall, school house, and post-office. Number of inhabitants about 100.

By Abram Price.

His father, William Price, emigrated to Ohio from Virginia in 1820, and died aged sixty years. My informant has served his township as treasurer for several years, and was a store-keeper in Lyndon.

By E. F. Coiner.

His father, Robert Coiner, emigrated from Virginia in 1836, and served for many years as justice of the peace and deacon in the Presbyterian Church, was sergeant of a company in the war of 1812; is now a notary public, and aged about seventy-six years.

By John Howard.

His father, Adam, emigrated from Rockingham county, Virginia, to Ohio, in 1809. He served as a soldier in the war of the Revolution, and died at the age of seventy-two years. My informant served one term as director of the infirmary of Ross county, and has lived in the township fifty-eight years. Old settlers, Joseph Warnuch and Leeman. Warnuch served as a soldier in the war of the Revolution. J. Ricketts served as a soldier in the French war. Anderson Bryan served in the war of the Revolution.

By William Tharp.

His father, Daniel Tharp, emigrated from Rockingham county, Virginia, in 1810, and died aged seventy-three years. My informant served as a soldier in the war of 1812, and at the time the war broke out, he was in Columbus, Ohio, making brick. He helped to make the brick for the old State House. He says in 1812 the place was but a village. On Mr. John Depoy's farm there has been, as is supposed, an ancient camp ground of the Indians, where many arrows of different sizes and shape may be found. In early days, on what is called the muddy fork of Buckskin, there was a beaver dam constructed across that stream, which remained, in part, for many years. Old settlers, James E. and Alex. Kerr, James Watt, Abram Stookey, Jacob Hire, John Fernour, John Sample (the latter was captain of a company in the war of 1812), William Grant, John Wallace, Robert Dubois, and James Dickey. Revs. Pittinger and Johnston were the first preachers. Mr. Tharp has an old-fashioned churn, which his family uses at the present day, and which is over one hundred years old. The churn is made from the wood of the cypress.

By Robert D. Patterson.

He was a carpenter, and moved from Highland to Buckskin township in 1841, and has served his township as constable for several years. He also served as one of the deputies for sheriffs Ghormley and Adams.

By Crawford Caldwell.

He emigrated to Ohio from Ireland in the first settlement of the country; served as a soldier in the war of 1812; has been a resident of the township for seventy years, and is now aged about eighty years. Old settlers, Jarret Erwin; William Smith, who served in the Revolutionary war; John McLean, also a Revolutionary soldier; Robert Holliday, who fought at the battle of Trenton, and Alexander Scroggs.

By John Lucas.

Ezra Lucas, his father, was born at Marietta, Ohio, and moved to Ross county in 1811. He was in the war of 1812, was a cooper, and died aged about seventy-five years. His grandfather, Isaac Lucas, was one of the first settlers at Marietta. He came from Boston, served seven years in the Revolutionary war, and was at the battle of Bunker Hill.

By Robert Wilson.

He was born near Pittsburg, in 1781, and from there he removed to near Wheeling, where, he says, he saw the body of the first person killed by the Indians near that place—a man named Robert Edgar. In 1797 or 1798 he moved to near Flemingsburg, Kentucky, and, in the fall of 1800, to Ohio, where he settled on Buckskin creek, near South Salem, on a farm his father had bought the previous year, when there were but three or four families living on the creek. In those early days, he says, the farmers turned their horses and cattle loose in the woods, to feast themselves on the luxurious herbage which grew so plentifully, and when they were needed they would have to be hunted in the deep forests, as they sometimes strayed many miles from home. On those occasions he invariably carried his trusty rifle for protection and to kill game. He also says that he has killed many bears in those hills, and sometimes when they were feasting upon some of their hogs. The bear will not take time to kill a hog before eating, but as soon as it is caught will commence devouring it, the hog squealing as long as he has life. He says he has often been attracted to the place by the squealing of the hogs and killed the bear. Sometimes the hogs would return home with the flesh all torn from their backs. The wolves were also very plentiful and destructive to the sheep and pigs. "I was in the woods," says he, "one day, when my dog came running to me much frightened, and I saw, in a few moments, five large wolves in full chase after him. I fired and succeeded in killing one, when the balance made their escape into the forest.

"Our cabin was often visited by the Indians, who encamped on the creek near us, for days at a time, to hunt game. In 1802, after Ohio became a State, emigration increased in our neighborhood, and we began to have religious services. The first sermon preached in Buckskin was in the woods, on my father's farm, near where Major Irwin's house now stands, by two Presbyterian ministers, named Marcus and Dunlevy. After the service was closed, Father Irwin arose and made a short exhortation, and closed by saying: 'These ministers can not live upon the wind, therefore I propose to take up a collection,' when taking up his hat he threw into it a silver dollar, and passing it around collected several dollars. The first church edifice erected was a small log building, near the residence of James A. Wallace. The first minister who remained any length of time was the Rev. Robert B. Dobbins, who was with us three or four years; the next was the Rev. James H. Dickey, who remained twenty-seven years."

My informant says: "I bought the farm I now live upon in 1804, and in 1805 did the first work on it; I cut the date—February 15, 1805—in the bark of a beech tree which stands near my residence; the tree is still standing, and the date is quite perceptible. In the same year, I planted some apple trees, which still bear fruit. I was married and settled on my farm in 1812, where I have lived ever since. In the summer of 1813, I was in the service of the United States as a soldier, having been called out to protect the frontier just after Fort Meigs had been besieged by the British, and was most of the time stationed at Lower Sandusky. I was a member of a rifle or light company belonging to a battalion commanded by Major Robert Harper. Before we were discharged, my brother-in-law, John Halliday, and myself had our horses sent to us to ride home, and we turned them into a large pasture near the fort, till the time of our discharge. Halliday went out one day to salt the horses, and, after having gone some distance in the pasture, he heard a noise behind him near the fence, and looking around saw a party of Indians making for him; he started back on 'double quick time.' After running about half way across the pasture, he looked over his shoulder and saw one large Indian in advance of the others, so close that he could see the white of his eyes, which gave renewed impetus to his speed. On nearing the fence he looked for a favorable spot to cross, and to his great joy he saw a place where there was a wide space between the top rail of the fence and the rider; he made for it, and, without touching the fence, bounded through into the thick woods, and eluded his pursuers, and making a circuit of some miles got safely back to the fort."

Mr. Wilson is yet living and quite spry; his age is about eighty-nine years.

By Colonel William Collier.

His father, Captain James Collier, was born in Dauphin county, Pennsylvania, May 20, 1752. When the colonies declared their independence, Mr. Collier took a decided stand in their favor. In 1776, he commanded a company in an expedition known as the Flying Camp; they rendezvoused at Lancaster, from there they marched to New York, took an active part in the battle of Long Island, and assisted in several skirmishes up the North river. They also fought at the battle of White Plains, and were with General Washington during his retreat through New Jersey. He also assisted in the capture of the Hessians at Trenton, and in 1777 was in the battle of Brandywine; also, was in several skirmishes at the White House. He and his company participated in the terrible sufferings at Valley Forge, where they were encamped for some time with General Washington. In 1778, Captain Collier was given command of a company by the authorities of the State of Pennsylvania, and ordered to Northumberland county to guard the frontier against the Indians. At Sunbury he joined a State regiment, and was stationed at Fort Muncie, on the west branch of the Susquehanna. He took an active part at the battle of Freeland's Fort. Having no command at this place, he volunteered to bring in the dead. In 1779, he received a commission to enlist a company of rangers to serve during the war, in which he continued until its close. For his gallantry he was presented by General Lafayette with a fine sword, which is still in the family.

In 1814, he came to Ohio from Pennsylvania, and settled in Buckskin township, where he lived till the year 1844, when death called him away, lamented and beloved by all who knew him.

Paxton Township.

Township Officers.

Justices of the Peace, J. M. Pearce and Charles Robbins; Trustees, A. W. Seymore, A. Ferneaur, and J. W. Ferneaur; Constable, Samuel Tweed; Township Clerk, Charles Robbins; Treasurer, J. H. Huling; Land Appraiser, Austin Pepple; Attorneys, A. O. Hewett, J. R. Whitney, Lee S. Estel, and S. M. Penn.

Officers of the Town of Bainbridge.

Mayor, Lee S. Estel; Marshal, William Rittenhouse; City Council, Charles Robbins, Samuel Townsend, Dr. S. C. Roberts, John H. Huling, and Robert N. Ivens; Recorder, A. E. McGoffin; Postmaster, A. E. McGoffin.

Number of Stores, etc.

Eleven stores and groceries, one drug store, three blacksmiths, two wagon-makers, two harness-makers, four shoemakers, two tinners, one silversmith, two tanneries, four doctors, one saloon, one pump-maker, one hotel, one boarding house, two barbers, one bakery, one butcher, one carpenter, two mantua-makers, two painters, one stoneyard, one Presbyterian and three Methodist churches (including one colored), one union school and one colored school, three parsonages, and one National Bank by Rockhold & Co. Number of inhabitants, 900.

By Elijah Rockhold

His father, Joseph Rockhold, emigrated from Pennsylvania to Ohio in 1797, and settled first at the Highbank Prairie; moved from there to Paxton township in 1800; served as captain of a company during the war of 1812, and his township for twenty-seven years as justice of the peace; he died at the age of eighty-five years.

Old Settlers.

Thomas and Captain William Stockton served during the war of 1812. Amos and Joseph Reeder. Christian Benner built the first iron works at the Little Falls of Paint creek; he emigrated from Germany to Ohio at a very early day. Henry Benner served as justice of the peace and captain of militia for many years. John Benner was born in Pennsylvania, and when but a small child, came with his parents to Ohio. Here he studied for, and was admitted to the bar, but soon left his practice, as his father needed his aid on the farm. He was a good neighbor, highly respected and loved by all who knew him. He died September 13, 1869, aged sixty-seven years. At the time of his death, he held the office of mayor of Bainbridge and justice of the peace. The first mill was built by Jacob Smith, at the Big Falls of Paint creek; first hotel was kept by John Torbett; first postmaster was Elijah Kelly, a blacksmith, who was also justice of the peace for many years. Mary Rockhold, mother of Elijah, is one of the oldest ladies in the county, being now ninety-four years of age. She is in good health, and retains her mind to a remarkable degree. The author was introduced to her one evening by her son, when he awkwardly addressed her: " Why, you are a pretty old lady." She answered: "I am old, but not pretty, and never was." She is now living with her son in Bainbridge. Mrs. Rockhold says one of the first hotels was kept by Mr. Christian Platter, who was also a miller. The first store was kept by Enos Folk.

By Jacob Gault, of Bainbridge.

Mr. Gault emigrated to Ohio from Virginia in 1790, and served in the war of 1812; his captain was Mr. Joseph Rockhold. Mr. Gault was at Hull's surrender, and at the siege of Lower Sandusky, under General William Henry Harrison; he served during the war; was afterward captain of a rifle company of militia. He went from Bainbridge to Kentucky, and drove the carriage that conveyed Henry Clay to his home in that State when on his return from the treaty of Ghent, and remained with that celebrated statesman and patriot eight days at his own mansion. Mr. Clay's wife and daughter, and a gentleman by the name of Brown, were in the carriage with them. Mr. Gault says Mr. Clay was a fine violin player, and they had quite a pleasant trip. Mr. Gault used to drive team over the mountains from Chillicothe to the East for goods for the Messrs. Campbell, in early days; he is now living, and over eighty years of age. He says in his younger days he was a little wild, which, of course, most men are. He relates the following as one of his boyish pranks: He was working at the old Reeves' tannery, two miles east of Bainbridge, and in the neighborhood there was a young lady and gentleman who were engaged to be married. The day had been set and all the usual preparations made, but from some cause or other (my informant does not state whether his good looks had anything to do with the matter or not), the young lady repented, and, in her distress, applied to Mr. Gault and asked: "What shall I do? or where shall I fly?" He told her that in the cellar of the tannery, there was a large hogshead in which, if she wished, she could hide, and he would see that she was cared for, which kind offer the young lady accepted, and, together, they, on the evening when the twain were to have been united, hied off to the cellar, and the young lady, assisted by her gallant, entered the hogshead, when he covered it over with large pieces of tan bark, and day after day, for eight days, she remained in her prison-house, my informant conveying her food. On the evening of the eighth day, Mr. Gault procured a carriage and conveyed the lady to Lancaster, Ohio, and thus she eluded her would-be-husband.

From McDonald's Sketches, pp. 57, 58.

"In the year 1795, while Wayne was in treaty with the Indians, a company came out from Manchester, on the Ohio

river, to explore the Northwestern Territory, and especially the
valley of the Scioto. General Massie was in this little band.
After proceeding several days cautiously, they fell on Paint
creek, near the falls. Here they found fresh Indian signs, and
had not traveled far before they heard the bells on the horses.
Some of the company were what was called *raw hands*, and previous to this wanted much 'to smell Indian powder.' One of
the company, who had fought in the Revolutionary war, and
also with the Indians, said to one of these vaunting fellows:
'If you do, you will run, or I am mistaken.' A council was
now called. Some of the most experienced thought it was too
late to retreat, and thought it best to take the enemy by surprise. General Massie, Fallenach, and R. W. Finley were
to lead on the company, and Captain Petty was to bring up the
rear. The Indians were encamped on Paint creek, precisely at
what is called Reeves' Crossing. They came on them by surprise, and out of forty men, about twenty of them fought.
Those fellows who wanted to smell powder so much, ran the
other way, and hid behind logs, and Captain Petty reported
afterward that they had the ague, they were so much affrighted.
The battle was soon ended in favor of the whites, for the Indians fled across the creek, and left all they had but their guns.
Several were killed and wounded, and one white man, a Mr.
Robinson, was shot through the body, and died immediately.
These Indians had one male prisoner with them, who made his
escape to the whites, and was brought home to his relatives.
As soon as the company could gather up all the horses and
skins, and other plunder, they retreated for the settlement at
Manchester, on the Ohio river. Night overtook them on the
waters of Scioto Brush creek, and as they expected to be followed by the Indians, they made preparation for the skirmish.
The next morning, an hour before day, the attack was made
with vigor on the part of the Indians, and resisted as manfully
by a few of the whites. There being a sink-hole near, those
bragging cowards got down into it, to prevent the balls from hit-
ting them. Several horses were killed, and one man, a Mr.

Gilfillan, shot through the thigh. After an hour's contest, the Indians retreated; and the company arrived at the place they started from, having lost one man, and one man wounded."

By Samuel Peacock.

His grandfather, Martin Gilmore, was in the battle of Reeves' Crossing above mentioned, and in the fight became separated from the company; two Indians gave chase; he ran to where Reeves' mill stands, and crossing the creek, turned and fired on the Indians, killing one of them, and had the satisfaction of seeing his carcass float down the stream. The Indians fired on him several times, but did not hit him, and he finally made his way in safety back to his company. He moved from Amsterdam to Bainbridge, where he lived for many years. He raised one of the first cabins in the place, and carried on the tailoring business. John Thompson served a term of years as commissioner of Ross county.

By George Free.

His father, Frederick Free, emigrated to Ohio from Virginia at a very early day, accompanied with his family, including George, who has now been a resident of the township for sixty years. He was called out during the war of 1812, but furnished a substitute by the name of David McClellan. Near his residence was a stream called Cliff run, a branch of Paint creek, which, for natural scenery, can not easily be surpassed. Its banks in places rise to the hight of fifty or sixty feet, of solid limestone, almost perpendicular, and on the top are interspersed with pine, which give the cliffs a beautiful appearance. At the point where this stream enters Paint creek, and for two miles above, are also cliffs, on either side, of limestone, rising sometimes nearly one hundred feet, with caves extending from fifteen to twenty feet and of considerable dimensions. Mr. Free's wife was a daughter of William Warnick, who was a subscriber to the *Scioto Gazette* for fifty years.

By Joseph Ogle.

He emigrated to Ohio from Kentucky about the year 1800; was born in Maryland; was in the war of 1812 in Captain Joseph Rockhold's company; was a home hunter, and has killed many bear, deer, and other game. He hauled wood for the use of the first legislature, which convened at Chillicothe. He is now nearly eighty-eight years of age. His wife was a daughter of Abram Popple, who emigrated from Maryland to Kentucky, and from Kentucky to Ohio, in 1808. Her brother Abram was in the war of 1812. Old settlers, William Kent, Nathan Reeves, and John Ferneaur. The first preachers in the neighborhood were Rev. Wm. Mick and Rev. J. B. Finley. Mrs. Ogle says she has heard Mr. Finley preach many times. He used to preach to the Indians, and had a colored man to interpret for him.

By Joseph Platter.

His father, Christian Platter, emigrated from Kentucky to Ohio in 1800; served his township in different offices for many years; built the mill on Paint creek known as the Platter mill, and died aged seventy-seven years. Joseph has served as township officer in different capacities for many years. He says near Bainbridge is a bank of red clay which some of the neighbors have used for painting their buildings, supposed to be the same with which the Indians used to paint themselves at the Big Falls of Paint. The water pours over a solid limestone rock, and falls about eight or ten feet, and just below there is another fall, but not so great.

By Robert Dill.

His father Robert Dill, Sen., and Thomas Dill, emigrated, in the first place, from Pennsylvania to Kentucky. From there they came to Ohio in 1800, and erected one of the first cabins that was built in the township. Robert Dill, Sen., served as justice of the peace for several years. Indians were very plenty when they first came to Ohio, and would often call at their cabin. Mr. Dill was a home hunter. Deer were so plenty that they were often killed for their skins alone. At one time, while out on a hunt, he had quite a fight with wolves, there being some ten or fifteen of them, but escaped without harm. Mr. Dill, on making his first payment for his land, had to go to Pennsylvania. To make it, he started on horseback with about $1,500 in his saddle-bags, and on the way his horse, by some means, escaped from him, and started off with the money. After a hard chase and much anxiety of mind, he overhauled him and found all safe. Todd's trace passed immediately in front of the house in which he now resides. He has served his township as an officer in different capacities from time to time. His father died aged seventy-one years.

Ancient Works.

On Mr. Dill's farm are six ancient mounds, of different sizes, from twenty to thirty feet in hight, and on Mr. Richard Dill's farm is an ancient fort or fortification containing about twenty-four acres, which is a perfect square. The embankment is from three to four feet in hight, and, at regular intervals, there are low places or gaps. On Mr. Thomas Blackstone's farm is a circular formed work, containing some seventeen acres. The embankment is three or four feet in hight. All of these works seem to have been subjected to fire at some time, as there is found on them ashes and coals; pieces of earthenware, some of fine workmanship, have been found in and about them. Near some of these works freestone rocks, finely dressed, are found, some of them of an oblong shape, three by four feet, with the corners rounded off. One of these mounds is coated with gravel some eighteen inches in depth, and surrounded by a stone wall some three feet in hight. Several years since this mound was opened, and a skeleton was found in the inside, in a sitting posture, surrounded with stone.

By Thomas Blackstone.

His father, John Blackstone, emigrated from Virginia to Ohio in 1802, and was in the war of 1812. He was also at the defeat of St. Clair. During the fight he became very thirsty, and lay down to take a drink. Not knowing they were defeated, he was soon informed of that fact by another soldier, by the name of Black, who, when flying past and seeing him lying there, called to him and said: " Blackstone! d—— it, why don't you run?" He rose and found the whole army in flight. But he soon was up with them. He died aged seventy, two years. He was a great hunter, and killed many bear, deer, wolves, and other game. One of his neighbors went to a deer lick at one time, and saw what he supposed to be the ears of a bear through the brush, working back and forth, as though keeping off the flies, when he up with his gun and fired. When the gun cracked he heard the tingle of a bell, and, upon going to the spot, to his surprise he found, instead of a bear, his own yearling colt.

By D. C. Carson, of Bainbridge.

The first tannery in Paxton township was sunk by Nathan Reeves, two miles east of Bainbridge, at the crossing of Paint. He also kept a ferry boat at said crossing. Reeves emigrated from Virginia, with the Carsons, about the year 1798. Mr. Carson's father, Robert, settled in Highland county when New Market was the county seat, one mile west of where Hillsborough was laid out, where he sunk a tannery. The first school house was built on the farm of Christian Platter. It was also the first preaching place in the township. General Massie was one of the first settlers in the township, two miles west of Bainbridge. He laid out a town north of Paint creek, at the Great Falls, which was named Amsterdam. Here he built a grist mill and still house on the north side and a saw mill on the south. It was, however, very sickly, so he laid out Bainbridge, and it proving more healthy, Amsterdam was vacated. He also built a furnace on his farm, above town. Amos Folk was the first merchant in Bainbridge. He brought his goods from Chillicothe, in the first place, in saddle-bags. E. Kelly was the first blacksmith and justice of the peace. Austin Southard was the first shoemaker. These three families composed the town for two or more years. Massie's mills, still house, and furnace are all gone. D. C. Carson was born in 1799, in all probability the first white male child born in the township. There has been fourteen still houses built in the township, but at this time there are none. Near Bainbridge are two fine sulphur springs, very strong, and perhaps as good as any in the State.

By Mr. Howard Newman, of Twin Township.

On Mr. Price Taylor's farm, in Paxton township, stood a large mound, which Mr. Newman worked into brick some years ago. In this mound he found numerous human bones, some of a very large size, sometimes almost the entire frame. Some of the skulls were in a good state of preservation, containing the entire teeth. He found the center of the mound seemed to be filled with decayed matter, perhaps of human bodies; among this he found charcoal, pieces of lead, etc. Mr. Newman worked on this mound some three years before he made it up into brick.

Liberty Township.

Township Officers.

Justices of the Peace, Elijah Humphrey and T. B. Erskine; Trustees, Joseph Thomas, Madison Arganbright, and J. W. Drummond; Treasurer, Samuel G. Griffin; Clerk, Elisha Murphy; Constables, Thomas Grubb and Charles Parrott; Land Appraiser, Levi Jones; Postmaster, Thomas Ratliff.

The village of Londonderry contains about two hundred inhabitants, one M. E. Church, cemetery, two stores, three groceries, two hotels, five blacksmith shops, one school house, one saddlery, two shoemaker shops, one silversmith and gunsmith, three physicians.

For the above I am indebted to Mr. Samuel G. Griffin, father of Mr. P. G. Griffin, clerk of the court of Ross county. Mr. Griffin emigrated to Ohio from Virginia in 1831, and is now aged about sixty-nine years. He has served his township as treasurer for thirty-two years, and justice of the peace for several years.

Ancient Works.

On Mr. Thomas Orr's and Milton Jones' farms, near the bank of the Scioto river, is quite a large earthwork, several feet in hight, in an eight-square shape, with a gap at each corner. The inclosure contains about fifteen acres. On the same lands, near the river bank, is another earthwork, thrown up in a perfect circle, containing about twenty or twenty-five acres, with a lane or gap dug out leading down to the water's edge.

On Mr. Daniel Harness' farm is another of those ancient works, square shaped, and in the center is a small mound six or eight feet in hight, the wall containing within it about eight acres. Mr. Harness says on his farm, on the bank of the Scioto river, where the water had washed some of the bank away, were found at one time quite a large number of leaden balls of different sizes and shapes, some of them weighing an ounce or more, perhaps in all half a bushel, indicating that at some time there had been quite a severe battle there. He also states there was found on his farm a large stone pipe, weighing one pound, with the shape of a human face neatly cut upon it. Near the same place was found a marble or stone ball as large as a good sized apple, perfectly round and smooth, with a hole through the center, with many other curiously cut stones and darts. On Mr. Ed. Harness' farm is another of those mounds, which is about one hundred feet long, sixty feet wide, and fifteen to eighteen feet in hight. Mr. Harness says at one time some persons opened this mound, and the inside was found to be quite hollow, the cavity admitting a person by stooping a little. Around the base were found buried a great number of human skeletons of quite a small size. A number of them were dug out. Under the head of each skeleton were found the fibers of seemingly very fine cloth, the threads appearing very plainly. Near this mound is a curiously shaped earthwork thrown up, containing some ten acres within the walls, with a long lane or outlet leading out for some distance from the main work.

Mr. John Davis, whose name appears in another place in this work, says Mr. Harness, in early times, started to Chillicothe on horseback to buy some salt, just after he had settled where he now lives, taking with him the last dollar he had, which would pay at that time for a half bushel. On the way he met a party who proposed a horse race for one dollar a side. Mr. Davis put up his dollar and won the race, and with his two dollars he bought a bushel instead of a half bushel of salt.

By Simpson Jones.

Among the very first settlements made in Ross county was that of the Highbank Prairie, now included in this township. As early as 1798 corn was raised by different parties on that prairie. The crop spoken of by J. B. Finley, as having been raised by James Kilgore on the Station Prairie, was beyond doubt raised on the Highbank Prairie. As Kilgore settled and put up his cabin about where Horace Crookham now lives, and was living there in 1798, it is hardly likely he would cross the river and go up two miles to raise corn, when there was as good or better land within a few hundred yards of his cabin. Mr. Kilgore afterward bought the upper tract of the Highbank Prairie, and divided it with a Mr. Holton, on which tracts of land, now owned by Thomas Orr and Milton Jones, both of them ended their days. We have no information that Mr. Kilgore attempted to raise any crop previous to 1798, in which year he did raise corn on the Highbank Prairie; so that we conclude the first corn was raised by the whites on that prairie instead of the Station. Among the earlier settlers who came out to make a crop preparatory to a settlement, were Thomas and Zebulon Orr, who raised corn on the Highbank in 1798 or 1799; also, Robert Corhen, Benjamin Kerns, Amos Taylor, and others—indeed, this was the center of the settlement, and the bank east of this rich and fertile prairie soon became lined with cabins, and so continued up to the time of the land sale. As the Government sold no smaller tracts than a section, it was the purpose of most of these early settlers to club together and buy homes on this prairie. But on the day of sale, when these lands were sold, the crier, instead of naming them the Highbank lands, offered them as the lands lying at the mouth of Indian creek, and they were bought by Benjamin Kerns, Felix Rennick, and Joseph Harness, except the upper fractional section, which was bought by James Kilgore and Holton. This made a scattering of the pioneers then settled along the bank, most of whom fell back upon the flats or second bottoms and uplands—some even seeking the hills on account of health and game. I have had it, says my informant, from more than one of these old settlers, that

it was their settled conviction that there was bribery used in the
selling of the Highbank lands, but just who was accused I
never learned. *

Rich and productive as these lands were, there was a terrible drawback to their attraction in the shape of chills and
fevers. So prevalent was this disease that not a cabin or a family escaped for a single year; and it often happened that of a
large family there would not be a single well member to fur-
nish drink to the others. In such cases buckets would be filled
in the morning by those most able and placed in some accessi-
ble place, so when the shakes came on each could help himself
or herself. Had there been any seeming possible way of get-
ing back to the old settlements, from which these adventurers
had come, most, if not all, would have left the rich Scioto bottoms, with their shakes and fevers; but so it was, there were no
railroads or canals, or even wagon roads, on which they could
convey their disheartened skeletons back to their old home-
steads, with their pure springs and health-restoring associa-
tions. At the time of the year when a tedious land or water
trip could be made, there were enough of each family sick to
prevent any preparatory arrangements for such a return; while
in winter there were even more obstacles in the way than the
sickness of summer. Thus held not only by the charms of the
scenery, and the productiveness of the soil, but by the sterner
realities of shakes and burning fevers, few that came ever returned, but every year brought new neighbors.

---

* Who the party guilty of the bribery of the crier was, seemed to be
indicated by several circumstances that followed soon after the sale. The
first wheat raised on the Highbank was by Mr. Kerns, who was permitted
to get it harvested and stacked, soon after which it was fired in the night
and burned up. Among the first patches cleared in the upland by Mr.
Kerns was for an orchard. Before fully completing the clearing, and while
the log-heaps were on fire, Mr. Kerns had his apple-trees planted. These
trees were obtained at a considerable cost, as there were no nurseries yet in
this country. A night or two after the trees were all set out, and before the
remains of the log-heaps were gone out, some person or persons went and
pulled up every tree in the orchard, and laid the roots in the fire!—Jos.
Smith.

But to return to the land sale. There was a general feeling of indignation toward the fortunate possessors of the Highbank lands, and parties who had expected to procure homes there hastened to make sure of the next best lands within reach. The Orrs removed to Dry run, in an adjoining township; Robert Corben and Benjamin Hanson located on Walnut creek, near Mooresville; Amos Taylor, Thomas Jones, McClintick, and others located on Walnut creek, where they lived till the close of life. On getting possession of the corn land on the Highbank, one of the purchasers claimed rent from those who had raised crops, and all paid except Thomas Orr. Orr refused to pay rent for Congress land, and was sued by Benjamin Kerns, who failed to recover.

Very soon after the sale of the Highbank lands, all the better portions of the township were entered, chiefly by speculators and parties clubbing together. Few persons had the means to enter a whole section, or even a half section. All the land in the township, except the Highbank, was covered with a heavy growth of timber, such as white and black oak, hickory, sugar, poplar, beech, and walnut. To cultivate this land it was necessary first to clear it, which was a laborious job. Much of this timber, especially on Walnut creek, consisted of the finest yellow poplar, tall and straight, and many of them four and six feet in diameter. To get these trees out of the way required much labor, as there were no saw mills, stationary or portable, then, to work up those remarkable trees, but thousands of them were deadened and suffered to stand and dry a few years, then cut down and burned by using the smaller limbs and other timber as "niggers." To clear a farm thickly set with timber was a work of years, and was accomplished only by persevering industry.

The beauty of these forests as they then stood, interspersed with all the varieties of timber common to this country, can only be imagined; and there is not a single nook or corner in the bounds of this township that has not been despoiled, not so much by the "scythe of time," as by the "ax of progress." It

scarcely seems possible that so great a change could be wrought
in all our forests in seventy years as has already been. And
it seems scarcely credible that in the settlement of a whole
township, not one land owner could have had forethought
enough to have saved a ten-acre lot of timber in its natural
glorious state, with its magnificent poplars, walnuts, oaks,
sugars, grapevines, pawpaws, spice-wood, etc. Such a ten-acre
lot, as it once stood seventy years ago, would to-day be a greater
curiosity, and attract more attention, than the best thousand
acre farm in Ross county. I know, says my informant, broken
lands, that were covered with forests of sugar and poplar, interspersed with other varieties, which if they now stood as they
stood even fifty years ago would bring one hundred dollars per
acre, now not worth ten dollars per acre. Such has been some
of our improvements on nature and her adornments.

The great pervading element our pioneers brought with
them was destructiveness to trees, vines, flowers, and shrubs;
to wild beasts, from the fat bear to the little ground squirrel;
and from the wild turkey to the humming bird, the same hand
of extermination was extended.

Speaking of those grand old poplars, says my informant,
reminds me of one I but recently manufactured into plank,
turning out over eleven thousand feet of weather-boarding, besides some seven hundred feet of inch plank. To get this tree
to the mill it was cut into eighteen logs, the four main body
logs being split into quarters.

Next to the forests, the great attraction was the game of
this region—the bear, deer, and wild turkeys. It frequently
happened that great fat bears would be treed close to the cabin,
and as for deer any one acquainted with the paths and divides
could very soon find a white tail. Thomas Jones, my grandfather, raised a pet bear from a cub, taken when quite small,
which was, in his manners, decidedly an oddity. When grown
he was kept chained in the yard to a stake, around which he
had his circle and play-ground. There was one spot in that
circle that he never passed without putting his nose to the

ground and turning a somersault. No whipping or fighting him could so confuse him as to cause him to pass that sacred spot without this singular exhibition. After he had fairly matured he was killed for his meat, and to get rid of the trouble of taking care of him. They also raised a pet deer which was, in her way, also a curiosity. She would go out in the woods and make friends with the wild deer, and then start for home in company with her gentleman deer, who generally forfeited his life by his attentions, for no sooner was the pet belled-deer in sight than the gun and dogs were turned on the wild deer, when the tame deer would join the dogs in the chase, and rarely fail in capturing the deceived animal. At last the trusty deer was shot by mistake for a wild deer, having gone out without her bell.

Persons who once became accustomed to the use of bear meat often preferred it to any other meat. How much of this preference was founded in imagination was illustrated by an anecdote I will relate, wherein a certain Joshua Baltinger and John Rogers figured as regular bear hunters, as well as bear eaters. It happened on a time when the old pioneers were on a trading expedition to the Jackson salt works, that they put up for the night with Thomas Jones, who had but recently arrived, and erected his cabin, but had not formed a taste for eating bear. A day or two before the arrival of his old acquaintances he had gone into the woods and killed a large black sow, and skinned and cut her up in the same manner as though she was a bear, taking care to leave her feet in the woods. Being fat the carcass had all the appearance of one, so much so that my grandfather said to the person who helped him to kill and dress the sow, "We will call her a bear." So the word went round that Tommy Jones had killed a fine fat bear. Such of the neighbors as liked bear meat must have a fry, while those who could n't go bear meat could not be prevailed on to touch the "critter." Among those was Tommy Jones himself. As the two travelers were unsaddling, they espied the black skin hanging across a pole, and at once inquired what skin that was.

"A bear," answered Tommy, quickly. "Killed a bear, Tommy?" "O, yes; a fine fat one, too." Turning to Rogers, Baltinger says: "I told thee we 'd get some bear meat before we got back, and now here it is." No excuse could prevent some bear meat from being fried for supper that night. Forthwith the skillet began to "siz and friz," and the peculiar flavor of the bear to fill the cabin, greatly to the delight of the old hunters. "Now," says Baltinger, "can 't thee smell the difference, Tommy, between that bear meat and pork?" No pork, or any other meat, smelt like that bear meat. Thus the conversation went on while the meat was cooking, till brought on the table, when one of the old bear eaters, taking some meat and gravy on his plate, says: "I tell thee, Tommy, where the difference is between this meat and gravy and pork; thee may eat all the bear gravy thee pleases, and it won't rise on the stomach like hog meat gravy." To this Tommy only remarked that "the paws of the bear were enough for him, he wanted nothing to do with the gravy." Thus feasted on bear meat from the old black sow, the old bear hunters went on their way rejoicing, taking good care to call again on their return trip to get another fill of bear meat, nor were they informed of the joke for some months afterward.

At that time hogs would generally be fat in the woods. Scarcely a year but there were either acorns or beech-nuts, and always roots in abundance. Of wild turkeys there was a great abundance. When a boy, says my informant, I shot a wild hen turkey that weighed nineteen pounds, a weight I never have known a tame hen turkey to reach. From what I have seen of the wild and tame turkey, I am satisfied there has been no improvement made by domestication. On the contrary, I am satisfied there has been a perceptible deterioration in the turkey family since their domestication. The reasons for this I have nowhere seen accounted for.

Old Settlers.

Thomas Jones, my grandfather, emigrated from New Jersey in 1804, and settled on Walnut creek, where he opened a small farm, and raised nine sons and two daughters, all of whom lived to grow up, and all married and settled in the same neighborhood. For years he could take his nine sons into the harvest field, and himself leading with the hand sickle make ten hands. Each of his eleven children became the head of a numerous household. The old homestead is still retained, and is in the possession of the youngest child. The Abraham Claypool and Amos Taylor farms remain in the possession of the children. With these exceptions all the other lands in the township have passed from the original purchasers into new hands.

Jefferson Township.

By J. W. Vanmeter.

This township is in the southeast part of the county. Salt creek passes through it, near the center, in a southwest direction. Richmond is the only town in the township, situated on the west bank of Salt creek and on the road leading from Chillicothe to Jackson. The town contains about three hundred inhabitants, with five stores, two groceries, two hotels, two tanyards, two blacksmith shops, three wagon shops, and two shoemaker shops—all doing a good business; one fine Methodist Episcopal Church, one large school house, with a school of from one to two hundred pupils, one gunsmith shop, two physicians, one surveyor, and one harness-maker.

At the east end of the town is a fine flouring and saw mill and a woolen factory. The advantages of water power here are perhaps as good as any in the county. At the crossing of the creek there is a fine bridge.

East of the creek the land is hilly, where a chance deer may be seen; west of the creek the land is good. The township was settled originally by Quakers from North Carolina. The town was laid out in 1811 by the Moffitts. The Coxes and Hinsons settled at this place in 1798. Soon after the settlement, other settlers came—the Meekers, Strattons, Minears, and many more Connecticut Yankees; also, the Rittenours, on whose land is a stone barn, where the Rev. Mr. Cartwright preached in 1805. Anthony Rittenour emigrated to Ohio, from Maryland, at an early day, and has long since passed away, and his son Jacob is the only one of the name left, who is now about eighty-six years of age. Mr. Rittenour served his country in the war of 1812; he is the oldest man living in the township. Benjamin Short, aged eighty-four years, also served in the war of 1812—these two being the only old soldiers of that war now living in the township. None of the Moffitts, or their descendants, now live in the township, they having long since moved to Chillicothe, Illinois. Henry Hinson, an early settler, died some years since, aged eighty; his son, John Hinson, is the oldest man now living who was born in the township; he is aged sixty-five years. Eli Stratton, one of the first settlers, died in 1867, aged eighty-nine years, having lived in the same house fifty-three years; he moved to town about a year previous to his death. He was the father of S. D. Stratton, late recorder of Ross county. Out of all the persons living here forty years ago but five remain in the town and five in the township, all the others having died or moved away.

In this township are many old relics of the past, such as Indian graves, where charcoal, parched corn, fish bones, deer and dog bones, and whole human skeletons are found in the same mound, with plenty of broken earthenware, arrows, and pipes; and near the town at least a peck of large leaden balls have been picked up, and pieces of gun-barrels are also found, showing—as some suppose—the severe fighting old De Soto had, when on his way to Canada, with the aborigines. The old Indian trail, from Kanawha to Chillicothe, passes here, going by way of the salt works at Poplar Row, now called Jackson. Mr. Rittenour says he has seen at least one hundred squaws, with their pappooses fastened to boards, resting or camping half a mile from town.

This township was at one time famous for hunting, game of all kinds being in abundance, and occasionally, to this day, a deer runs through the town; and the season is counted poor if we do not kill at least a dozen rattlesnakes in the township.

Mr. John Griffis, an old settler, who carries on the tannery which was erected in 1825, is now seventy-one or seventy-two years of age. He has been a resident of this place fifty years.

Besides other things, we claim to have the tallest man in the county, Mr. J. A. Stancliff, whose hight is six feet seven and a half inches. In the first settlement of this township, we had the social evil in the shape of still-houses. We had three in town, and nine within a mile of the place. My informant says he has seen nine fights in half an hour, where the blows fell fast and furious; when all was over the parties would scramble up with mashed noses and black eyes, repair to the first doggery, and drink friends until the next meeting. With all this we have had but one person sent from this township to the penitentiary, and none hung as yet.

In this township, between the years of 1821 and 1847, there were twelve deaths by drowning, to-wit: Captain Levi Hicks, two names unknown, Lorenzo Moffitt, a Mr. Dawson, John Hagans, a Mr. Martin, Peter Burr, two children of J. Tomlinson, Anson Graves, and Daniel Bailey.

Deerfield Township.

Deerfield township is noted for its large and extended plains, and rich and fertile bottoms on the Scioto and Deer creek, the ancient park for the elk and deer. Clarksburg, in this township, derives its name from Colonel William Clark, a veteran of the war of 1812, who resided on Hays creek.

Township Officers.

J. W. Timmons and A. S. Holloway, Justices ; James Templin, Clerk ; E. W. Templin, Treasurer ; Samuel Cochran, Peter Baker, and J. W. Hurst, Trustees ; O. M. Hinson, Assessor ; James Templin, Jr., Land Appraiser.

Early Settlers.

Captain Clement Brown emigrated, in 1802, from Delaware. In 1803 he married Miss Rachel White, and permanently settled on the land which he had purchased on the rich bottoms of Deer creek. Mrs. Rachel Brown, his mother, came out that year, with the rest of her family—White, Henrietta, Kethura, Zaccheus, and Mary. John Wiley, who afterward married Henrietta, came out with them. Captain Brown cleared his land and cultivated it until 1812, when he and his company went to Fort Seneca, under Colonel Clark. On his return he continued the cultivation of his farm. He died at the age of eighty years, and such had been the increase in the value of land, that that which had cost him but little, was, at the time of his death, considered worth $200,000. He left a son and a daughter, Thomas W. and Sarah. Thomas W. Brown lives on his farm of two hundred acres at Mount Pleasant. He owns, beside, two thousand acres at other places. He has served his township in various capacities, as trustee, assessor, etc. His family consists of Richard N., N. W., Ambrose, Sina, Rebecca, Richard P., Rachel, Elmore, and Kate W.

White Brown erected the first mill in the township. He was an exemplary man, a class leader in the Methodist Episcopal Church for many years, and the father of Methodism in Deerfield township. He died, much lamented, in 1841, aged ninety-one years. His family consisted of Rebecca, Lucian, Amelia, Elizabeth, Anna, Margaret, Nelson, Mary, William, Sarah, Francis, and Priscilla.

Edward Tiffin, a relative of Governor Tiffin, emigrated to Deerfield in 1803, and located on the Scioto. He served in the war of 1812. He married a daughter of White Brown, and they had the following children : Mary Ann, Milton, Martha, Cynthia, Margaret, and Edward ; by his second wife he had three children—Newton, James, and Isabella.

Rev. Lorenzo Dow preached in White Brown's barn in 1828. Rev. Stephen Timmons, who emigrated to Deerfield in 1802, was the first Methodist preacher on Deer creek. He served several terms as justice of the peace, and was an early advocate of anti-slavery. He raised a large and respectable family. Abraham Shanton emigrated in 1803, and was in the war of 1812. Nathan Hide was a man of some note and popularity in the county. He was representative in 1865, and held, at various times, important township offices. He moved to Illinois. Colonel Hegler was in the war of 1812, as was also George Hill, a farmer and hunter. Samuel Clark was a son of Colonel William Clark. William Bryant, C. P. Davis, H. Ransom, P. H. Potts, and William Goldsberg were farmers ; William Stagg, a noted panther hunter ; Abram Payne, a singular man, but good company. William Haggard, who died at the age of eighty-three years, and M. Bragg, a farmer, were in the war of 1812. Jacob Switzer, Jacob Robinson, Daniel Counts, Len. Counts, Isaac Fleming, and James Miner were in Captain Brown's company in 1813. Levi Noble emigrated in 1800.

He was a noted hunter, and was in the war of 1812. His father served in the Revolutionary war. Abram Alter, Jacob Lister, E. Hide (who served thirty-three years as justice), and Thomas Hardy, were all in the war of 1812. J. H. Hervey, Ives Wagill, and William Kerkendall were early emigrants—about 1801.

Colonel William Clark, a farmer and tanner, was an early settler in Deerfield. He commanded a regiment of militia several years, and was at Hull's surrender. William Lister was an early pioneer; he served in the war of 1812; is now ninety-seven years of age, and voted at the last election. Joseph Timmons, son of the Rev. Stephen Timmons, the old pioneer preacher, is a man of ability and influence; he is now a justice of the peace. John Foster came to Deerfield in 1802, and was the first school teacher in the township. His sons were Charles, John, Andrew, and James. John and James Tuttle owned large farms on Deer creek; were men of influence and wealth, and early settlers in the township. David Jones was chaplain to General Wayne, in 1793–95, and Andrew Jones was one of his spies. Colonel Evans was in the Revolutionary war; came here in 1796. John McNeil. J. Wise; died aged one hundred years. Frederick Bray, Indian killer, died aged ninety-one years. Persal Smith. Joseph Conrad; had at one time three wives; died aged ninety-nine years. Byron and Baron Leffenwell were soldiers in the war of 1812. William Pennell was a fife-major under Colonel Clark. Thomas Carney and S. Howell were pioneers in 1801. Henry Mallow, George Smith, M. Stites, B. Thomas, Henry Lawrence, Robert Taylor, and Elwell Brown were mechanics, farmers, and merchants, useful citizens, and early emigrants. Benjamin Grimes, Curtis Williams, James Tender, Thomas Junk, David Hagar, John McCarthy, M. P. Junk, Amos Scropes, William Jones, Michael Bush, John Bush, S. Mangold, John Farlow, David Plilly, Edward Young, C. Stratton, Martin Peterson, John Holloway, G. Vincent, John Junk, Henry Colsten, J. Clemens, Aaron Beatonham, Lemuel Holloway, Thomas Carney, S. Chester, and Rufus Betts were all early pioneers, and nearly all in the war of 1812.

James Templin, Sen., emigrated from Kentucky to this township in 1795. His family consisted of Solomon, Robert, Jeremiah, Isaac, Margaret, and John. He landed at Portsmouth, and came up the Scioto to the station. He bought his land from General Massie. Old Town was then the headquarters of the Indians. He and his brother John were in Colonel Clark's regiment in the war of 1812, and helped build Fort Meigs. At the close of the war he resumed the cultivation of his farm. He was twice married, and had fourteen children. He is now eighty-one years of age and rather feeble. His children are scattered, most of them being in the West.

The following pioneer names were handed in by Captain Hoddy: Lieutenant John Jackson ; James Huffman ; Noah Downs, fifer in Captain Brown's company ; James Baker, drummer ; Rev. P. Baker, first Baptist preacher and father of Peter Baker ; Edward and Thomas Noland, Stephen Emory, and Uriah Betts. The above were all farmers, and were in Colonel Clark's regiment.

Colonel William Clark's staff, in 1812, were : Robert Hoddy, Adjutant ; Benjamin Grimes, Chaplain ; James Miner, Paymaster ; William Clawson, Quartermaster ; John Clark, Sergeant-major ; M. E. Peterson, Lieutenant-colonel ; and Major Calloway.

Colerain Township.

Township Officers.

Washington Jennings, Andrew Hinton, and Samuel Haris-
inger, Justices of the Peace; Jacob Bonstoer, S. Pontious, and
Andrew Hinton, Trustees; John May, Clerk; A. Rose, Treasurer;
J. Throgmorton, Assessor; Andrew Wiggins and A. G. Betzer,
Constables; David Jones, Land Appraiser.

Colerain township, in early days, was a noted place for
game of every kind. Walnut and Salt creeks were headquarters
for all the hunters in the neighborhood; their high and craggy
banks were the hiding places of bears, panthers, and wolves.
The township is watered by the head waters of Walnut, Salt,
and Kinikinick creeks. The face of the country is part rolling
and part level; the soil is rich, and every acre can be tilled.

Adelpha is the principal town in the township, and is
one of the oldest towns in the State. It has several stores,
churches, etc.

Old Settlers.

Hon. Daniel Kershner was the first pioneer settler in this
township, having come in 1796. He had quite a large farm, and
was a man of some prominence. He served as captain in the
war of 1812, and represented the county in the legislature in
1836. He died in 1844, at the age of eighty-four years. He
had three sons—Daniel, John, and Elisha. Daniel, Jr., married
and settled at the head waters of Walnut creek. He was
captain of the militia, served two terms as county commissioner,
and held several township offices. He is now seventy-two years
of age, in good health, and much respected. John, the second
son, is owner of the old stone fort and a farm on Salt creek.

He married a daughter of the late Colonel Spangler; has held several township trusts. There are several mounds and one old fort circle on his farm. Elisha, the third son, lives near John; a good farmer and excellent neighbor. John Kershner, Jr., is a bachelor, a great land speculator and stock dealer. The Kershners are all great land owners, men of wealth and influence.

Hon. Elias Henton was one of the earliest pioneers. Prior to leaving Virginia he had been elected judge. He was a noted hunter as early as 1796. The last panthers and bears he killed were in 1805, on the waters of Walnut creek. He held the office of justice for twenty-one years, and has served his township in other capacities. He is still living, much respected by his numerous friends and relatives. Aaron Jones has taken a great interest in improvements; is a man of sterling principles and sound sense. He was justice of the peace many years. Moses Jones was an early pioneer; entered his land in the forest, and made it a fine farm; held several civil and military offices, and was a man of character and highly respected. Martin Dresback was a pioneer of 1798. He was a soldier in General Harmar's campaign of 1791 and a noted hunter. He died at the age of ninety-six years. John Bookwalter was an early settler in Salt creek valley; a good hunter. He served as spy from 1783 to 1795, in the campaigns against the Indians. He died at the age of ninety-five years, and his wife, Barbara, at the age of ninety-eight. Joseph, Aaron, and William Bookwalter were among the early pioneers, who cleared their farms in the forest wilderness and braved all the dangers of frontier life. They were men of worth and enterprise. William is still living on his farm, a useful citizen. John May was a pioneer of 1799. He was a great hunter, and served in the wars of 1791 and 1812. Frederick Pontious was an early settler; a good man, who had much influence in society. He served several terms as justice. Washington Jennings was an early emigrant, a good farmer, and quite popular. He was a justice for many years. Joseph Poland, Henry Strauser, Isaac Harper, Isaac Larich, George

Flanagan, Jacob Boucher, and Conrad Rudy were all early pioneers, and came at the same time. Captain John Patterson was one of the first settlers of Colerain, a brave, energetic man. His father was a major in the Revolution. He served as a captain in the war of 1812, and was several terms justice of the peace. He died eighty years of age. Major Engle, a brave and kind man, and a good farmer, earned his title in the war of 1812. John Dunn was a farmer and justice; a noted man. Saml. Harisinger emigrated at an early day; a farmer; has served several years as justice and postmaster at Adelpha. David Kershner built the first distillery in the township. John Beach was the first innkeeper, and Alexander Smith the first shoemaker. Peter Marshall established the first boot and shoe store in the township. John Stelinger was the first carpenter, Martin Nungester the next; Barton O'Neil, the first blacksmith and carpenter. Flanagan Merriman, an early settler in Colerain, is yet living, at the age of eighty-one years. Nathaniel Throgmorton, an early pioneer, has a large farm; a man of sound sense, in whose opinion his neighbors place great confidence. He is one of our best citizens, and has raised a large and respectable family. Peter Goodman, a great stock dealer, David Holderman, Conrad Betzer, John Brown, Peter Strauser, Anthony Betzner, and John Strawner were all early pioneers. Samuel Dresback, an early settler, a man of influence, and full of enterprise, has held several township offices, and is much esteemed. John Alenather, Henry Hickel, T. W. Hickel, Frederick Haynes, Andrew Haynes; George Gower, an English soldier under Dunmore, from whom Fort Gower took its name; Moses Dawson, David Dawson, Thomas Arnstow, William Hoover, J. D. Smith, D. Jones, Jacob Strouse, Thomas Nutter, Thomas Patton, Jacob Alexander Jacob Grawutt, N. Justin, Peter White, Peter Nicol, and Noah Clark were all early pioneers—all dead but three, and their descendants scattered over the West. David C. Bolous, the hermit, was an Indian killer and bear hunter. He came to the Hocking caves, from the Kanawha region, in Virginia, in 1789. He was never married, having been disappointed. Here he lived alone in the dense forest, and hunted game, which was in abundance. He would take the skins, furs, and venison to the Ohio, and sell to the traders. In 1791 he shifted his quarters to near Fort Harmar, and from there went, as a spy, to the Maumee, with General St. Clair, and was taken prisoner by the Indians, and lived with them until Wayne's treaty in 1795. He came to old Daniel Kershner's in 1797, and stayed there till the fall of 1799, when he went to the old earth fort on Salt creek, and built a cabin there, in which he lived till the time of his death in 1802. He had killed, in his time, ninety-six bears, seventy-three wolves, and forty-three panthers.

Ancient Mounds, etc.

On John Kershner, Jr.'s, farm is a model mound, thirty-five feet high; and on the west bank of Salt creek, an earth fort, in the shape of a half-moon; one large gateway, and a circular earthwork, extending from the half-moon to the ancient earth fort.

Union Township.

In Union township the face of the country is rather un-
even. The bottom lands on the Scioto and Paint and Deer
creeks are rich, and produce corn and grain of the best
quality. Deer creek divides the township into North and
South Union. The streams running through South Union are
Robinson's run, Anderson's run, Acton's run, Menary run, and
Musselman's run, all emptying into Paint creek. The following streams empty into Deer creek: Yellow run, Dry run, and
Hay run.

*Early Settlers. By John Robinson, President of the Ross County
Pioneer Association.*

His father, Joshua Robinson, emigrated to the Scioto Valley
in 1795, in company with General Nathaniel Massie and his
surveyors. On arriving at the station near where Chillicothe
now is, they proceeded up the main Paint creek. Following
the Indian trail at Reeves' Crossings, they came suddenly upon
a party of Indians encamped. A battle ensued, which soon
ended in favor of the whites. The Indians retreated through
the woods, carrying off everything but their guns. Joshua
Robinson was shot through the body and died immediately.
The body was interred near the mouth of Rocky fork, at the
head of the rapids. A white man, who had been prisoner with
the Indians, made his escape during the fight. The party retreated to the Three Islands. William Robinson, brother of Joshua,
was also in this fight. He bought six hundred and forty acres
from General Massie in South Union, four miles south of Chillicothe. He moved to his purchase in 1800, and erected the first
cabin in the vicinity, and soon cleared a fine farm. When the
war was declared in 1812, he was one of the first to volunteer,
although over age. He died at the age of seventy years. John
Robinson, on the death of his father, was adopted by his uncle

William, and lived with him till he was of age. He was corporal in Captain Alexander Menary's company, of Colonel Clark's regiment, and marched to Sandusky. When the war was over, the regiment was disbanded at Chillicothe, and Mr. Robinson settled on the land on which he still lives, eighty-three years of age, in the enjoyment of good health. He had three sons, James, John, Jr., and Joshua—the latter dead—and two daughters. He furnishes us with the following names of early settlers: William Wilcox, William Cochran, Richard Bradley, Alexander McClintock, B. Johnston, M. Yates, M. Dolly, M. Robertson, Alexander Robertson, and J. Clark, who all served in Colonel Wm. Clark's regiment in the war of 1812.

John Acton, a man well advanced in years, came to Ross county in 1810, with his family, viz: Richard, John, William, Jeremiah, Sarah, and Benjamin, and settled in South Union. Richard and John were noted hunters. They died in 1810, aged respectively eighty-nine and eighty-eight years. William was in Captain Menary's company during the war of 1812. After it was over he settled on Colonel Evans' land. He is now living on his farm on the north fork of Paint creek, eighty-two years of age, and in good health and spirits. He furnishes the following names of early settlers: James Weaver, who is the father of ten sons, all farmers; Jacob Shedy, James Augustus, Oliver Michael, James Anderson, James Pool, Michael Musselman, William Rogers, James Duncan, Jr.; General James Menary, who served in the war of 1812, and one term in the legislature; Richard Atherton, L. H. Atherton, Henry Atherton, and John Anderson, who was in the war of 1812.

Names of Early Settlers, furnished by Major James Weaver.

William Pool, Jacob Sharer, S. Organ, Oliver Nichols, Revs. Joseph and James Nichols, Addison Nichols, Stephen Ryan, Daniel Beard, George Steel, T. Anderson, Charles Binns, John Guster, James Steel; Richard Barrett, blacksmith; T. Arthur, first merchant and preacher; H. Rouse, Wm. Fulton, Wm. Noble, and S. Day, who were all farmers.

Names and Records, by John N. Hurst.

His father, Levi Hurst, and family emigrated to Ross county, from Maryland, in 1801. They came in one-horse carts to Wheeling, where he purchased a flat-boat, in which he floated his effects to Portsmouth, except the horses, which were sent by land. Here he hitched up his carts again, and in nine days reached Chillicothe, in the month of June. He moved into the woods the September following. Wild game was very plenty, and the Indians were hunting in great numbers that fall, so that clearing progressed very slowly. Mr. Hurst was the father of eight children. His sons' names were James, William, Harper, Samuel, Thomas, and John N. The latter occupies the beautiful homestead on Dry run. He has served his township as justice, clerk, assessor, etc. They are all Methodists. General Hurst, who served in the late war, and is now United States revenue collector, is a relative of 'Squire Hurst. When Captain Harrod was killed by the Indians, a company was raised and pursued them as far as Old Town. In returning they indulged in firing at game, which so alarmed the settlers that they all left their cabins, and the whole thirteen families collected at Levi Hurst's, expecting an attack. Mrs. Hubbard stood during the night near the window, with an ax, saying that she would kill the first Indian that would attempt to get in. Mr. Levi Hurst built the first hewed log-house in the township. He was born in 1770, and died in 1861. He and his wife had lived together seventy years.

John Rogers, one of the pioneers, helped to build the first cabin in Chillicothe. He was in the valley three months prior to the arrival of the first white woman, and drove the first cattle from Kentucky to Chillicothe. His old cabin is still standing. Judge James Armstrong served as judge one term. He was a man of ability. Joseph Clark, James and Hamilton Rogers were early settlers. Judge Joshua Robinson died in 1862, aged eighty-eight years. Thomas, John, and Joseph McCoy were the first settlers on Dry run. Thomas Earl was

an early settler and good man; served as justice several terms.
David Augustus was in the war of 1812. Joseph Counts, John
Russell, Henry Davis, and William Harvey were the first school
teachers. Rev. Benj. Young was the first preacher. Rev. H.
Smith organized the first Methodist Church in 1800. The first
camp meeting was held in 1803, on Thomas Watts' farm. Eben
Timmons, Thomas Hicks, Thomas Willis, Robert Harvey, T.
Tootte, N. Adams, Isaac Cook; James Dunlap, who was a mem-
ber of the State legislature; Colonel Evans, a man of great
enterprise and a large land owner, who came from Kentucky;
Philip Miner, Jacob Mace, Joshua Clark, Joseph Counts, Asa
Hawkins, Jacob Crispin, Levi Warner, Abram Winder, Charles
Fryson, John Hinder, Milton Anderson, Thomas Thompson,
Mr. Williams, David Corbit, Michael Baily, William Fulton,
and Daniel Beard, who was in the war of 1812.

John Dunlap, father of James and all the other Dunlaps in
this region, emigrated to Union township in 1796, and was so
much pleased with the Scioto Valley that he bought a large
body of land on the west bank of the Scioto, for which he gave
nineteen cents an acre. This land is now owned by his sons,
and is worth one hundred dollars per acre. His wife was a
granddaughter of Dr. Benjamin Franklin. His sons were
Robert, Rufus, James, John, Major, and Lorenzo.

Casper Smith came to the Scioto Valley in 1796. His
father was a captain during the Revolutionary war. Casper
was in the war of 1812, and died in 1845. Henry and Thomas
Bowdell and James Fish came in 1800. Rachel Buckworth is
yet living, and has raised a large family. Thomas Vinsant.
Mr. McCarfity, an early settler, was in the war of 1812. The
latter was a kind man and good neighbor. His widow is yet
living at Chillicothe, and still owns the old farm. John Huber,
Sen., John Huber, Jr., and Henry Russell, all farmers, with large
families. John Robinson, Thomas Littleton, Joseph Charge,
Henry Cook, John Davis, Thomas Earl, Caleb Leland, and
John James came in 1799; all farmers.

Pioneer Names, etc., by Michael Beaver, Jr.

Michael Beaver, Sen., emigrated to Ross county from Virginia in 1800. His family consisted of Michael, Joseph, Eliza, Susan, and Elias. He purchased a section of the military land on Deer creek. He served in the Revolutionary war, and his son Michael in the war of 1812. The wife of the latter died in 1860, aged seventy-nine years. Peter Jackson was a justice for several terms, and had been in the Revolutionary war. John Baker, John Kirkendal, and Stephen Timmons. The latter was the first Methodist preacher, in 1796. William Noble still lives, at the age of eighty-eight years. A. Davenport. B. Rhinehart's sons, John, Jacob, Henry, and Abel, are prominent and useful citizens. They were early settlers, having come in 1796. Jacob was a captain in the war of 1812, and his brothers were all members of his company. Abner and Benj. Kerns were drovers in the war of 1812. Colonel John Mace and Andrew Mace were sons of Jacob Mace, an early pioneer. This family have occupied prominent positions in civil and military affairs. J. S. Mace is now sheriff of Ross county. He is a man of influence and an efficient officer. John Thompson, Jesse Grimes, Hezekiah Ingham, Isaac Ingham, and James Whitesides were in the war of 1812. George Bennett was the first blacksmith, and Len. Warner the first potter. William and Isaac Warner were carpenters. The Warner family were Quakers. Philip Mencil was a captain in Colonel Clark's regiment. This regiment was mustered out in 1813, on the farm of M. Beaver, on Deer creek. Anson Watts, who was also in that war, is still living, eighty-five years of age.

Ancient Works.

On Mrs. Steel's farm is a large earthwork, with two miles of wall, several large mounds, squares, gateways, and bastions. There is a circle on Mr. George Shearer's farm a mile long, with embankments six feet high. There is a large mound and circular fort on Mr. Wood's farm.

Harrison Township.

Township Officers.

James T. Search and Hiram Creamer, Justices; Frederick Wheeland, L. Freeman, and John Strauser, Trustees; Samuel Nichols, Treasurer; James Search, Assessor; Warren Walters, Clerk.

On the east side of Walnut creek, adjoining Hocking county, the country is mountainous, with narrow valleys between. The prominent sugar-loaf peaks, covered with the evergreen spruce and cedar, were as late as 1805 famous hunting grounds for bear, panthers, wolves, wild cats, foxes, elk, deer, wild turkeys, and smaller game. Black, racer, copperhead, rattle, and garter snakes were very abundant. Mr. Hanson killed a racer which was sixteen feet long. Big Foot, the Indian chief, called this the bad ground—the habitation of bad spirits. It was considered unsafe to travel through it either on foot or horseback unarmed. It was a noted hunting park for both the Indians and the white hunters. The township is thickly settled along the valleys of Walnut and Sugar creeks. The high hills are too steep to cultivate, and the soil too poor to produce profitable crops. Walnut creek is twenty miles long, rising in Colerain and emptying into Scioto river.

Early Settlers.

Samuel Hanson and family, who emigrated in 1798; Louis Graves, George Stanhope, James and Bennett Arinesly, Joseph Vangrundy, George Bishop, Daniel Ream, Anthony Raypole, John Lewis, Joseph Farmer, George and John Robuck, William Johnson, Andrew Thompson, William Lockard, John Ortman, Stephen Ross, Thomas Hanks, James Carothers, and Samuel Nichols were all early pioneers of Harrison township.

The following were in the service during the war of 1812: Colonel Wm. Johnson, Captain Abram Moore, Major Abraham Lewis, Drum-Major John Ortman, Lieutenant George Stanhope, Edward Satts, Abner and Thomas Ezra, Joseph Vangrundy; Samuel Moore, still living, aged eighty-eight years; Joseph Moore, John Young, Joseph and John Hanks, Daniel Ulm, A. Raple, Lawrence Russell, and Hugh Dalahan.

Mr. Aaron Syms informs us that the great abundance of game in this region drew to it daring hunters from all parts of the country, and especially Kentucky. Major A. McClundy, the companion of Boone and Kenton, visited this region in 1778, and made his headquarters at the old earth fort. The second day after he arrived his dog Sago started up a monstrous he-bear, and immediately attacked it. The bear seized the dog, and started off with him, hugging him with a tight grasp. The major followed, and when near enough to shoot without injuring the dog, fired, but only wounded the bear. The enraged animal now dropped the dog, and made a desperate attack on McClundy, who, after a severe, close fight, succeeded in killing him with his knife. During a hunt of ten days on the waters of Walnut and Salt creeks, McClundy killed thirteen bears, nine wolves, six panthers, and three wild cats, besides other game.

Springfield Township.

Township Officers.

Joseph Smith and Aaron Elliott, Justices; Leonard Moore, Andrew J. Cryder, and Thomas McNeal, Trustees; Warren Senff, Assessor; Joshua Seney, Treasurer; Jacob Cryder, Land Appraiser.

Early Settlers—East Springfield.

In 1805, Thomas and John Arthurs, and Thomas McNeal, Sen., emigrated from Brooke county, Virginia, and settled in East Springfield. Thomas Arthurs' family consisted of two sons and one daughter. Samuel, the eldest son, served in the war of 1812; Thomas, the other son, was a lieutenant in Captain Wall's company; they are both living. Mr. McNeal's father came from Scotland, and was a lieutenant in the Indian wars after the Revolution. All of the family moved West, with the exception of Thomas, his oldest son, who is still a resident of this township, and all are now dead; their names were Nancy, William, Samuel, and Jonathan. Thomas is now eighty years of age, and has served his township as trustee and justice several times.

The Indian traces were plain in this region in 1805, and many arrow heads and stone axes are yet picked up in the fields. Mr. McNeal says he has often counted as many as eighty Indians in a squad, passing through from Old Town to Salt and Raccoon creeks to obtain lead and hunt. They generally returned with their pouches full and their horses loaded.

Many of the early pioneers were noted hunters. Garrett Boots, Philip Walden, Elisha Carpenter, Henry Hershaw,

Joseph Taylor, Martin Overly, C. Neff, George Boots, Leslie Malone, Daniel Ducher, John Cummins, James Caruthers, William Pendleton, James Useley, and B. McNeal were all famous hunters and trappers.

The following are the pioneers who came to this township before the war of 1812:

Adam, Alexander, and Joel McClintic; T. Jones, Samuel Hershaw, Benjamin Deamons. Amos Taylor, Daniel Armstrong; Zachariah, Isaac, and Samuel Welsh; James and Samuel Kilgore, Andrew Young, Thomas Wilkins, Caleb and William Odell, Joseph Harness, Felix Renick; James, Henry, and A. Cartwright; Philip Argrebright, Jacob Shane, Geo. Patmore, Thomas Orr, William Zebulan, Thomas Hanks, Zachariah Linton, Hugh and Michael Dalihan, Benjamin Carnes, Philip and Stephen Roos, Aaron Doll, Peter Yeaker, James Redman, Francis and Richard Malone, Leonard Neff, Edward Satts, R. Murphy, A. Claypool, and Benjamin Hilton.

Colonel Sifford, a resident of West Springfield, though not a pioneer, was an early settler, and a man of influence and enterprise. He is now a representative from Ross county, and has served as United States marshal, county surveyor, and commissioner, and has held other important trusts.

The first duel (so called) fought in the Scioto Valley was in 1793. While the pioneers were exposed to the attacks of Indians, a stockade fort was maintained at the old station on the Scioto as a place of retreat. One morning, John Vanasaw, a noted hunter, shortly after leaving the fort on a hunt, saw an Indian rise from an ambush, decked and painted in war costume. Both raised their rifles to their shoulders at the same time, and fired. The Indian fell, and Vanasaw, fearing there might be other Indians about, returned to the fort and reported his *duel.*

Casper Senff, grandfather of Michael Senff, emigrated from Germany in 1773. He was a king's hunter, and served as a spy in the Revolution. Michael came to Ohio in 1803, served in the war of 1812, and died in 1845. His sons were Michael,

Jr., Jesse, Andrew, George, and John. Michael, Jr., owns the old farm, and is a great fruit grower.

There are two streams in East Springfield, Dry run and Lick run, and one sulphur spring.

Early Settlers—West Springfield.

Michael Cryder, Sen., served as commissary in the Revolutionary war, and emigrated to the Scioto Valley in 1796. He brought with him his wife and six sons, John, Henry, Michael, Emanuel, Jacob, and Daniel, all remarkable for their size and physical strength. They settled in what is now West Springfield; all are now dead, and few of their descendants living. About the same time, Henry Musselman came from Kentucky to the Scioto, and erected the first mill on the river, for many years the resort of all the neighboring settlers. He was one of the first justices in the valley, and owned the land where Hopetown stands, and gave it that name. He died at the age of eighty-five years. Jacob Mace and John Cryder emigrated in 1788; were relations of Michael Cryder; some of their descendants are still living. Jacob Weider came from Pennsylvania in 1799, and settled near Hopetown, where he lived and died, aged eighty-eight years. His family are all dead or gone West, except Mrs. Julia Downs, who still lives in the township. Mr. Weider was proprietor of a tavern and distillery at Barley Forks, now Hopetown. Frederick Overly came to the Scioto Valley in 1797, and his son John still lives on the old farm. Barton Overly came at the same time. Zachariah Jones came to Scioto in 1798, and is still living, in the one hundredth year of his age. Alexander, Samuel, and Daniel McRoberts, Archibald McFarland, George Wheeland, and Philip Hines emigrated in 1800. Zachariah Jones, Samuel McRoberts, David Cryder, and Jacob and Isaac Innell served in the war of 1812.

Ancient Works.

In Springfield township are many old forts, mounds, and circles. One fort, containing some twenty acres, has walls ten feet high, with gateways on three sides. The north side is inclosed by a circular embankment not quite so high. The gateway on the south side has two embankments, forty feet apart, reaching down to the river. At a number of places in the inclosure, holes in the earth seem to indicate where wells had been dug. Many axes, arrow heads, animal teeth, etc., have been found here.

The celebrated Mount Logan is in this township, overlooking the Scioto river and Chillicothe. It was named after the celebrated Mingo chief, Logan, and is a great resort for celebrations, picnics, etc. The view from it is one of the finest in the valley.

Green Township.

Before Pickaway county was organized, Green township took in all the Indian towns on Sippo and Congo creeks. Major John Boggs' land was all in Ross county until Pickaway was organized. He was an early pioneer to the valley, having emigrated from Pennsylvania in 1796. His father, Captain John Boggs, served during the Revolution, and at the close of the war he moved and settled at the mouth of Boggs run, opposite Boggs Island, below Wheeling, on the Ohio river. He raised his family here until 1798, when he sold his land and descended the Ohio to Portsmouth. He then ascended the Scioto in a keel-boat to the station near Chillicothe. From there he traveled on foot to look after land. After traversing the valleys of the Scioto, he selected his land at the foot of the Pickaway plains, now known as the Crouse and Renick farms, and erected his cabin near the elm tree, noted as the spot where Logan delivered his celebrated speech in 1774. John Boggs, Jr., went back to Wheeling and married, and returned to his new home, where he cleared the land given him by his father. In 1803 he shipped the first flat-boat of flour to New Orleans. When the war broke out in 1812 he went as captain, but was soon promoted and served during the war as major. He lost his first wife, and married, for his second, the widow of Captain James Taylor, of Zanesville, Ohio, and died soon after his return to his old home. He was the last of the first pioneers on the plains, and was the father of nine children—William, Martha, Lemuel, John, Nancy, Moses, Lydia, James, and Sidney. James is the present owner of the farm, and has erected a circular board fence around the Logan tree. The farm is dotted with ancient mounds. One, on the north bank of Congo creek, measures one thousand feet around and is thirty feet high. On the land entered by Captain Boggs, in 1796, were the Indian towns called Squaw Town, Cornstalk Town, and Black Mount, all on Sippo creek.

James Boggs, son of Major Boggs, was killed by the Indians while on a hunting excursion with several young men on the Stillwater. William Boggs, brother to the Major, was taken prisoner by the Indians in 1793, and kept as such until Wayne's treaty with them at Fort Greenville in 1795, when he was released and sent home. On his arrival there he was dressed in Indian costume, and his father did not know him at first sight. He left, but returned next day and made himself known, and, like the Prodigal Son, was kindly received by his father, who exclaimed, " This, my son, who was lost, now is found ; was dead, but now is alive."

John Boggs was an Indian spy, and well known by them ; they often waylaid him in order to get his scalp, and disliked him because he was a brave, fearless scout and forest ranger. They often made William run the gauntlet, and on one occasion he had to run seventy-five yards and jump into a hut, in the door of which they had placed a large squaw to keep him out ; but he, knowing what he had to do, started, and was pushed very hard, the squaw standing in the door. He struck her with his head, and knocked her clear across the cabin and almost killed her, the Indians laughing themselves almost to death at her expense and calling him a brave man.

The following names of early pioneers were handed in by Rebecca Wolf, daughter of Captain Wolf, who was eleven years old when her father settled on Congo creek in 1796 : James Burns was in Hull's surrender. Mark Clark, John Shark, David and Samuel Demery, George Fry, Thomas Single, and William and Matthew Ferguson were all farmers, and served in the war of 1812. John Crouse built the first mill on Kinikinick creek, and was a man of enterprise and a useful citizen. John Clernson, the first postmaster, died aged ninety years.

Dr. Edward Ostrander was the first physician. Hugh Little was in the Revolution in 1776. John Liebery, Daniel Godman, J. Entricher, John Saxe, Thomas McGrody, William Dresback, John Eyestone, Benjamin Mark, J. Hedge, Elias Moore, Benjamin Steel, Samuel Evans, Dr. Shannon, W. S. French, J. Pepper, O. Justice, Abram Jones, John Gay, George Smith, M. Morgan, M. Price, Samuel Forkins, William McCoy, James Rogers, J. Bardles, were all early pioneers. M. Ferguson was the first distiller, and Henry Neil the first merchant. Hugh Forseman, James Torbett, William Beston, John and Joseph Creston, Samuel Knox, David Hare, John and James McMurphy, William Snodgrass, J. Young, Jacob and John Sailor, Caleb, James H., and J. Bush, George, James, and M. Rieke, George Frybark, Thomas Duncan, John McDonald (Indian trader), Isaac, Richard, and James Morris, Henry Hueston, Thomas Emerson, Thomas Barr, David Thomas, Abram Claypole, Isaac Brink, Jacob Leeding, E. Reed, D. Stark, John Snider, B. Midshore, L. Steely, James Burns, Eli Maschell, John Grimes, A. Jones, and Thomas Lingeral were in the war of 1812. H. May, A. Pontious, N. Wilson ; M. Slipes, the first mail carrier ; William Hamilton ; C. Dennison, the first tavern keeper ; Samuel Hill, John Dresback, M. Gruger, M. Godrich, Jacob Wagner, John Young, Henry Bell. The above-named first pioneers were brave and hardy men, a majority of whom were farmers. But few are now living. Perhaps Rebecca is the last of the pioneers of 1796.

Captain George Wolf emigrated with his father's family to the Pickaway plains in 1796. Captain Philip Wolf was an Indian spy during the Revolutionary war. After arriving at the plains they entered their land on Congo creek, on the tract on which Colonel Lewis camped in 1774. George Wolf went out as captain of a mounted rifle company, and marched to Upper Sandusky. After the close of the war he returned home and cultivated his farm till 1859, when he died. His second wife is still living. Captain Philip Wolf was the father of nine children—Mary, George, John, Elizabeth, Joseph, Rebecca,

Catherine, James, and John. Rebecca Wolf is the only one of the family now living. She lives on the old farm, and never was married. Franklin Wolf, son of George, is living on the part of the old farm where Colonel Lewis camped. Captain Wolf's children by his first wife were Mahala, born in 1804; Elitha, born in 1808; John, born in 1810; George, born in 1812; Harrison, born in 1813; Emerson, born in 1815; Franklin, by his second wife, in 1835. Mrs. Captain George Wolf is now living in Kingston; she is seventy-three years old, but enjoys good health and good company.

On the farm of the late Captain Philip Wolf, near the waters of Congo creek, is the place where the Indians got their lead. The mine has not been found, but large pieces of lead have been picked up. In 1860 Henry Wrench found a piece weighing over a pound, nine-tenths of which were pure lead. The mine is supposed to be within the limits of Colonel Lewis' encampment on the waters of the Congo, which flows through a fertile valley and empties into the Scioto. In this valley is supposed to exist one of the richest veins of lead in the State. A celebrated chief among the Delawares proposed to discover the mine to Philip Wolf for a given sum, but he declined the offer. Along Congo creek was the Indian trail. Starting at Old Town, it went in a southeast direction to Grandier Squaw Town. It left Black Mount and Cornstalk Town to the north. Both these towns were situated at the foot of the plains. The Indian trail, after passing through Camp Lewis, went on to Mount Logan, and from there to Fort Gower on the Ohio.

On the land of William Snodgrass was the Indian grave-yard. It is a mound one hundred and fifty feet in circumference and fifteen feet high. It was dug into by John Young in 1830, and skeletons exhumed. The mound is half a mile south of Colonel Lewis' camp, and close by the ancient Indian trail leading from Old Town to Fort Gower.

Captain Slover was taken prisoner at Crawford's defeat, and was condemned to be burned at the stake; but through a kind Providence, he was released and made his escape. He was confined in a death-house at Grandier Squaw Town, with two Indians to guard him. He loosened his bonds while the sentinels slept, got out of his cell, stole an Indian pony, and made his escape to Wheeling. He told the people of Wheeling that it was the best pony he ever rode; he never parted with it. Colonel Lewis expected to give the Indians battle at their towns on the waters of the Sippo and Congo, but the second conflict was prevented, Governor Dunmore overtaking Colonel Lewis in person, and turning him back when the Colonel was in sight of these towns.

Captain William McMeahen, a Revolutionary veteran of Virginia, had two horses stolen by the Indians. He got on their trail and followed them to Squaw Town, where he saw his horses. The Indians were out on a circle hunt, but he met a squaw that could talk broken English, who told him where the horses were, but advised him not to take them, as the Indians would kill him. She concealed him in her cabin and fed him until the Indians returned home. She then made a way for his escape. When he arrived at Wheeling his wife had gone home to her father, believing that he had been killed by the Indians. He told the people that he had never seen so fine a country; that the scenery and the richness of the soil surpassed all description, and that he was impressed with the belief that some of his posterity would, at no distant day, become occupants of those fertile plains and beautiful and wide-spread valleys on the Scioto, and his impressions were verified. The widow of Major Boggs was his daughter.

Concord Township.

The territory of Concord may, in truth, be called classic ground. Here, for past ages, the different Northwestern tribes of Indians annually met to hold their convocations; here once burned their council fires; here the clear, shrill voices of their chiefs, braves, and orators could be heard; here was their ancient home in times of war and peace—Old Chillicothe. But they have disappeared. Old Town, their ancient metropolis, has passed into the hands of the pale faces, and is now called Frankfort. Concord township is generally level, and the soil rich and productive. It is watered by the North fork of Paint creek and its tributaries. Harrod branch and Old Town run are the principal branches in the township. Paint creek derived its name from a Delaware chief; it heads in Madison county, flows through a fertile valley, and empties into Paint river near Chillicothe. At Old Town the allied tribes collected in 1774, marched forth and met Colonel Lewis, and fought the memorable battle of Point Pleasant, and after their defeat in this battle, they returned to these fields, collected their forces, and took their stand at Old Chillicothe. This was their strong position in their mode of warfare, and here they prepared themselves in anticipation of the enemy, or "Long Knives," to make a desperate struggle for their country and their town. The second conflict was prevented by Earl Dunmore crossing the Pickaway plains from Camp Charlotte and heading Colonel Lewis, when the Colonel and his royal army had arrived in sight of two of their towns on the east side of the Scioto and on the east side of Congo creek. Here, in person, Governor Dunmore turned Lewis back, he having made a treaty with the chiefs and agents under a large elm tree, the spot where Logan delivered his celebrated speech. This tree was fenced in, and is carefully cared for by James Boggs, the grandson of Captain John Boggs, the original owner of the noted farm and son of the late Major John Boggs.

Records of Pioneers.

Dr. D. Miller, grandfather of Dr. D. A. Miller, was a surgeon during the Revolutionary war under General Rufus Putnam, and witnessed the battles of Brandywine and Cowpens. John Miller, his son, was born in Maine, and emigrated to Marietta in 1806, and settled on one of General Putnam's farms on the Muskingum. He moved to Athens in 1810, and in 1812 he, with his company, was ordered out in the general call. He was a noted hunter. Daniel A. Miller, his son, an early emigrant to the Scioto Valley, resides in Roxabell, and is a successful magnetic physician.

The following names of early pioneers were handed in by Dr. Miller: Hon. Jesse P. Shepherd, a merchant; he represented Ross county in the legislature, and made a good member. Jacob Pancake, the first innkeeper, was very popular and extensively known; he is now living retired on his farm. Jacob Fisher emigrated in 1800; a farmer. Jacob Fisher, Jr., a farmer and hunter; killed a she-bear and three cubs on his own farm, and also a large panther and other game; he was a Presbyterian, a good man, useful citizen, and much beloved. Jacob Briggs was an early pioneer; a large farmer; a Presbyterian; a man of enterprise and energy. Captain Harrod, an early pioneer to Ross county, by occupation a farmer; he was a captain of militia. His brother, General Harrod, was in the war of 1812; his father, Major Harrod, was in the war of 1776, also under St. Clair in 1791. Captain Thomas Harrod was killed by the Indians while plowing his corn near the mouth of a tributary of Paint creek. The creek from that time was called Harrod's creek. A company of men pursued the Indians to Old

Town, on the Little Miami, but did not overtake them. On
their return they fired at game, which so terrified the settlers
that they all retreated to block-houses. The Indians, in 1773,
took Colonel Daniel Boone prisoner near the Three Islands, and
got him within seven miles of Old Town, when he escaped.
General Simon Kenton and Captain Slover run the gauntlet at
Old Town in 1788, also at Squaw Grandier and Cornstalk
Towns. Captain Wesley McGinnis, Lieutenant John Westhart,
Captain H. Mener, and David Carr run the gauntlet in Old
Town in 1794. Westhart, who died at Watertown, said Old
Town, in 1794, had over one hundred wigwams in it. Captain
Slover says in 1783 it had some two hundred cabins and huts.
Samuel Willy and J. Johnson were the first constables; David
Anderson, first treasurer and clerk of Concord; James Souther-
land and Fletcher Goldsberg were early pioneers and useful
men. F. Wells says Captain Thomas Harrod was killed by a
white man in 1802, and was buried at the mouth of now Harrod's creek, near the Bloomington road. Benjamin Goldsberg,
who served in the war of 1812, under Colonel Wm. Clark.
Robert and James Stewart, A. Robison, Berry Sane, and Benjamin Sane, aged ninety, who killed three bears in 1798, and Peter
Shannon, were all in the war of 1812; Robert Galbreth, first
merchant, T. Rittenhouse, second; John and H. Haynes, Morris and Wm. Latta, and John Fetters were all farmers; Rev. R.
Finley, first M. E. preacher; Rev. J. Carothers, first Presbyterian
preacher. Adam Mallow was a major, and H. Mallow a captain,
in the war of 1812. F. Mills, Esq., aged seventy-three, J. W.
Connel, Charles and Samuel Briggs, Samuel Johnson, Henry
McAdam, Wm. and James Cochran, Isaac Pancake, Wm. Rows,
Robert Stiner, Wm. Anderson, Wm. Cupper, G. and William
Haws, John Bush, Isaac Story, Charles and N. Primit, Wm.
Dixon, and T. McBolster were all farmers and stock merchants.
Mrs. Mary Branick is one hundred and eight years old, lives
three miles north of Frankfort, blind and very feeble; her
husband, Nehemiah Branick, and his brother Philamon, were

soldiers of the Revolution. Felix Wells emigrated from Kentucky in 1799, with his father's family, to Virginia, thence to Scioto Valley in 1800. When of proper age, Felix was elected justice of the peace, which office he held fifteen years. He is now seventy-three years old; his father's name was Francis Wells. N. W. Bush, aged ninety-four. John Templin was in the war of 1812, aged eighty-three, still lives. William Stagg, and John McNeil, aged eighty. Thomas Somerset emigrated from Kentucky to the Scioto Valley in 1796, and died in Frankfort in 1834; he served in the war of the Revolution; his son, Henry Somerset, was in the war of 1812. The descendants of the old veteran of the Revolution live, with few exceptions, in Ross county. David Maddox, Thomas Robinson, and Levi Corgold were in the war of 1812. John King was in the war of 1812. Elihu Wheeler, Ephraim Watson, James Dennison, Richard Donahue, and David Dooly were in the war of 1812. Milton Acton, John Acton, and Wheeler Andrew were all farmers and excellent citizens. Frederick Berley, chief Indian spy in Earl Dunmore's war of 1774, the Revolutionary war of 1776, and Indian war of 1791. He was a noted hunter—his home in the deep forest, his lodgings in caves, dens, and rocks; he possessed a strong constitution, suiting the time in which he lived, and was a hermit by choice. He killed, during his life, one hundred and sixty bears, ninety-six panthers, one hundred and six wolves, one thousand elk and deer, eleven buffalo, and other game in proportion; also ninety-six Indians. He was, during his excursions, often in company with the noted Indian spies, Kenton, Boone, Wolf, Boggs, Slover, Hughes, and Wetzel. He died in his cabin, aged one hundred and one years, on the waters of Mohegan, where a plain, and substantial monument was erected to his memory. He was taken prisoner three times by the Indians, and run the gauntlet at Sandusky, Squaw Town, and Old Town, in 1794. Peter Putnam emigrated to the Scioto Valley in 1796 to look at the country. Being much pleased with the rich bottom and plains of Paint, he returned to Hampshire, and brought his family out in 1809. His family consisted of Mary, Catherine, Elizabeth, Sophia, Peter, Jr., Joseph, Jacob, and Phillip.

Geneology of the Putnams.

Major John Putnam was born in Buckinghamshire, England, February 23, 1574; his father, Captain Philip Putnam; his grandfather, Colonel Peter Putnam ; his great-grandfather, Wm. Rufus Putnam ; his great-great-grandfather, Edward Putnam, of Putmanshire, England, A. D. 1194. The emigrant to America, Major John Putnam, brought with him three brothers, Thomas, Nathaniel, and Elisha, and two sons, William and Edward. They, as a colony, settled Salem, Massachusetts, November 20, 1634, where they all established themselves as successful farmers, and many of their posterity still live there. General Israel Putnam and General Rufus Putnam were the great-great-grandsons of Major John Putnam, who died in the one hundred and seventh year of his age. Generals Israel and Rufus greatly distinguished themselves in the French and Revolutionary wars. Edward Putnam, son of Major John Putnam, emigrated to Hardy county, Virginia, in 1662. The original name of the family was Puttenham, but in 1294, it was changed to Putmam, and at Salem, in 1635, changed to Putman. Still a portion of the descendants of Edward retain the name of Putman.*

The above is an extract from Cutter's Life of Putnams, published by Coolridge & Brothers, Pearl street, New York, in 1847.

Peter Putnam lives on his farm on Indian creek; Philip is living on his Greenfield farm. Their children are living in the county in good circumstances. Joseph and Jacob are dead.

---

* There is a tradition that the Putnams emigrated from Frankfort, Germany, to Putmanshire, England, about 998. All the Putnams in America descend from John Putnam, the pioneer of 1634, at Salem, Massachusetts.

Names of Pioneers handed in by Peter Putnam.

Rev. Nathan Cory, first Baptist preacher. Stephen Cory, Nicholas Debolt, C. McElroy, M. Emmit, and Joseph Morse were all in the war of 1812. William V. Vinsant was a justice twelve years. George Vinsant, Daniel and Jacob Shob, and Andrew Cochran, all farmers and mechanics, were also in the war of 1812.

There was a block-house on William Cochran's farm. Colonel A. Hagler commanded the militia in 1812. He was in the legislature two terms.

Captain Robert Hoddy emigrated to the Scioto Valley with his father's family, from Harper's Ferry, in 1790. Richard Hoddy, father of Robert, served in the Revolutionary war. Chillicothe had but one cabin when Richard Hoddy landed there, and that was covered with bark. Two thousand Indians from Old Town were encamped on the bank of the Scioto, where the upper bridge crosses that river. The first Territorial legislature met under a sycamore tree in 1797. Richard Hoddy entered five hundred acres of land, four miles from Old Town, on Paint creek, where he built the first flour and saw mill in the valley. He died in 1830.

Captain Robert, after the death of his father, took a load of flour to New Orleans. He erected the first distillery in the valley. In 1812 he served as adjutant under Colonel William Clark, and after the war he was elected land appraiser, assessor, and tax collector. Captain Hoddy is still living on his old farm, enjoying good health, and is now eighty-nine years of age. He married Peter Putnam's sister, Elizabeth, by whom he has had several children, all now living in the county.

Captain Hoddy served as commander-in-chief over the British prisoners after the war, until they were released. He was present at the shooting of the six militiamen. Captain Hoddy was well acquainted with Captain Philip Wolf. He says a braver man never lived.

"Rocky Mountain," as he called himself, emigrated to

Paint Valley at an early day, and erected his cabin, eight by
ten feet in size, near the mouth of Harrod's creek.   He said he
had been a spy under General Clark, in 1782, in his several
campaigns against the Indians; that he and Colonel Zane
served as spies for Colonel Crawford in 1783; that he belonged
to Colonel Lewis' legion in Lord Dunmore's campaign ; that he
served under Washington as a spy, and was under General
Harmar in 1791-2; that he was spy for Lewis and Clark during
their exploring expedition over the Rocky Mountains; that
in his war and hunting excursions he had killed Indians,
panthers, bears, buffalo, wolves, elk, deer, and smaller game
without number.   He possessed a pleasant disposition, was pro-
verbial for his honesty, and dressed very indifferently.   The
neighbors visited him to take him provisions, which he would
accept with a smile.   He never was married, having in his
youth been disappointed in his first love, which was the cause
of his choosing a hermit's life.   He would work for his neighbors when called on, and continued to do so until advanced age
incapacitated him for labor.   He emigrated from Virginia, in
1805, to the place already described.   At the time of the breaking out of the war of 1812, he was too old to serve.   In politics
he was a zealous Jefferson Democrat; in religion a Universalist.
He never failed to attend elections.   At the advanced age of
ninety-nine years, he died alone in his cabin, his faithful dog
alone witnessing his last moments.   At his own request, he
was buried on the top of the hill which overlooks his cabin.
Recently his remains were removed by kind friends to the
Bush Cemetery, and a plain monument tells the place where
rests the Rocky Mountain hermit.

Mounds and Ancient Works.

There are two large model mounds on the farm of the late
Captain Goldsberg, from which have been exhumed skeletons,
war implements, beads, arrows, etc.   On Jacob Briggs' farm
are several mounds, etc., and one near Old Town.

There is a large Indian graveyard near Old Town, and numerous skeletons have been dug from small mounds by laborers on the different pikes while taking out gravel for the roads.

Names of the Creeks and Runs in the Township.

North Fork, Little Paint, Harrod's creek, Greenland creek, Dry run, Squaw Lick, Hoddy run, and Indian creek.

Scioto Township.

Scioto township takes its name from the Scioto river, which runs through it. In early times, keel-boats and smaller craft ascended the Scioto to the station, which was about three miles below where Chillicothe now is. Some years ago, during very high water, a steamboat made a trip from Portsmouth to Circleville, and returned in safety. It created quite a sensation among the quiet denizens of the valley.

Before the completion of the Ohio canal, boats loaded with flour, etc., descended the Erie to New Orleans. These boatmen were a rough class, and sometimes, when a number of them were collected together, they would set the authorities at defiance, but taken all in all they were trustworthy and good-hearted. If goods were injured or lost, they were always ready to give full satisfaction. They were ever prompt in a quarrel to espouse the cause of the weaker party, especially of old men or strangers. The pioneer preachers held them in high estimation, and had great influence over them.

Chillicothe.

The town of Chillicothe, in Scioto township, was made the seat of government for the Northwestern Territory in 1800, which was previously at Cincinnati, but by act of Congress removed to Chillicothe. It was incorporated as a town January 4, 1802, and the following officers appointed by General St. Clair, commanding the Northwestern Territory :

Samuel Finley, Edward Tiffin, James Ferguson, Alexander McLaughlin, Arthur Stewart, John Carlisle, and Reuben Adams, Members of Select Council; Edward Harr, Assessor; Isaac

Brink, Supervisor; William Wallace, Tax Collector; Joseph Tiffin, Marshal.

The records of the town from this time till March 1, 1819, must be hid away or lost, as they are not to be found with the balance.

March 1, 1819, Levin Bett was Mayor; John Waddle, Treasurer; George Nashee, Recorder; Jacob Eichenberger, T. V. Swearengen, James Barnes, David Kinkead, and R. Souther-land, Members of Common Council.

The tax duplicate contained two hundred and twenty-two houses, two hundred and seventy-seven cattle, and other prop-erty, amounting in the aggregate to $538,295, and a tax of one-third per cent., assessed to pay the current expenses of the corporation.

In November, 1820, a disastrous fire occurred, which caused the organization of a fire department, which, as will be seen, was pretty extensive for that early day. Thomas James was appointed director; William Carson, Edward King, Robert G. Wilson, and William McFarland, assistants; Joseph Kerr, cap-tain of the bucket men; James Clifford, first lieutenant; Wil-liam Creighton, Jr., second lieutenant; John McCoy, captain of the property guard; John McLandburgh and James Miller, lieutenants; James Phillips, captain of hook and ladder and ax company; Richard Long, Adam Reister, and James How-ard, lieutenants. It was made the duty of the marshal to appoint citizens each night to patrol the streets and prevent confusion in time of fire.

Chillicothe was incorporated as a city April 9, 1838, and an election for city officers ordered, which resulted in the choice of William H. Skerritt for Mayor; Amasa D. Sproat, Treas-urer; Robert Adams, Recorder; Jacob Wolfe, Assessor; and Councilmen as follows: First Ward—John Leggitt, long term; J. A. Fulton, short term. Second Ward—John Wood, long term; William R. Drury, short term. Third Ward—Thomas Orr, long term; Levi Anderson, short term. Fourth Ward—James Howard, long term; James S. McGinnis, short term.

John A. Fulton was elected President of the first City Council. Robert Adams declined accepting the office of Recorder, and Thomas Ghormley was elected in his stead. James McCollister was elected City Marshal; Ebenezer Tuttle, Clerk of Market, and John Carlisle, Jr., Weighmaster, by the Council.

There has been no change in the corporation line since that time, while the suburbs have been rapidly increasing in population, and are now so densely populated that they should be annexed to the city proper. Present population, nine thousand.

The Pioneer Business Men of Chillicothe—By Rev. Dr. S. Mc-Adow.

Below I give you, as near as I can recollect, a list of the majority of the professional and business men of Chillicothe in its early days:

Ministers—First Presbyterian—Robert W. Finley, William Speer, Robert G. Wilson.

Associate Reformed—Samuel Crothers, John McFarland, Joseph Claybaugh.

Methodist Episcopal—Edward Tiffin (local), E. Harr (local), William Swaysey, Abdel Coleman.

Episcopalian—Messrs. Kellogg, Bosman, Peete.

Physicians—Samuel McAdow, Edward Tiffin, Joseph Scott, John Edminston, Samuel Monett, Crocker & Kennedy, Buell, Pinkerton, Hays, Atkinson, Wills.

Lawyers—Jessup Couch, Henry Brush, Thomas Scott, Joseph Sill, Richard Douglas, Edward King, Benjamin G. Leonard, William Creighton, Jr., William K. Bond, William S. Murphy, Michael Baldwin, Frederick Grimke, Nathan Sawyer.

Editors—John Collins, —— Richardson, James Barnes, Nashee & Denny, John Andrew, John Bailhache.

Clerk of Court—Humphrey Fullerton.

First Postmaster—William Creighton; first deputy, Ebenezer Tuttle.

Registers of the Land Office—Thomas Worthington, Jesse Spencer.

Druggists—Amasa Delano, Ira Delano.

Surveyors—Cadwallader Wallace, John A. Fulton, Allen Latham, Matthew Bonner.

Chillicothe Bank (first bank established in Chillicothe) *Officers*—First president, Samuel Findley; first cashier, William Sterrett; second president, Thomas James; second cashier, John Woodbridge.

Merchants—John McDougal, George Renick, John McCoy, Thomas James, John Whitesides, John McLandburgh, John Woodbridge, Nathan Gregg, Thomas Gregg, McLaughlin & Kinkaid, Robert Dun, James McClintick, William McDowell, Samuel Tagart, Barr & Campbell, Isaac Evans, Samuel Brown, George Brown, Ephriam Doolittle, William McFarland, Waddle & Davidson, W. R. Southard, William Ross, William Carson, Nimrod Hutt, William Irwin, William Miller, S. & F. Edwards, Craighead Ferguson, Samuel Ferguson, Benjamin Eaton, J. B. Andrews, Thos. Swearingen, Samuel Swearingen, O. T. Reeves, James Miller, John Wood, George Wood, James Culbertson, Smith Culbertson.

Fruit Merchants—The first fruit merchant was a man named Bebier, or Bebien, and following him came John Sherer. Here I will remark that Mr. Sherer went to the State of Pennsylvania, purchased his fruits, etc., shipped them to Portsmouth, Ohio, and from thence had them boated up the Scioto river to Chillicothe in his own keel-boat, and he always had plenty of fruits, both green and dried.

Hotel Keepers—Benjamin Umsted, Captain Lamb, Forest Micker, Green H. Lee, Adam Haller, Adam Betz, John Hutt, Thomas Cohen, John McCann, Edmond Basey, John Runkles, Stephen Cissna, Captain Beach, William Fitch, John Watson, James Phillips, John Madeira, Shaler Ives.

Tanners—Adam Turner, Nathan Reeves, —— Mantle, William Young, Samuel Brown, John McClean, Ely McKenzie, Thomas Jacobs, William Robbins, George Armstrong.

Cabinet Makers—John Kirkpatrick, William Kirkpatrick, —— Hume, William Robinson, Robert Robinson, John L. Tabb, Joseph Shepherd, Jonathan Miner, John Johnson, John Snyder.

Nail Manufacturers—I. Cook, Joseph Miller.

Cotton Factories—Hector Sandford, Ephraim Doolittle.

Woolen Factories—Moses Trader, Abraham Thompson, Levi Anderson, John Wilson.

Oil Mills—Thomas Davidson, W. Ross.

Book Binders—John Hellings, Richard H. Boyer, —— Foster.

Stone Cutters—George Meech, James Guin.

Silversmiths—John Cellers, Peter Spurk, James Gates, E. P. Pratt.

Candle Factories—Robert Long, William Morrow.

Weavers—John Philip Ott, Hugh Ghormley, John Wilson.

Grist and Saw Mill—David B. McComb.

Plasterers—James English, —— Barton, John Ferree, Joshua Evans, Jeremiah Beall.

Wagon Makers—John Robey, J. Myers, Thomas Hilliard, James Wright.

Coopers—Morris Fowler, Titus Marsh, James Wright.

Windmill Manufacturer and Cabinet Maker—Henry Baker.

Brick Maker—William Downs.

Clerks in Land Office, Stores, Banks, etc.—Winn Wynship, Sam'l Williams, Jos. Tiffin, Oliver Simpson, Capt. S. Leffingwell, Henry S. Lewis, Samuel Campbell, James P. Campbell, James S. Scranton, Austin Buchanan, William H. Douglas, George Tallman, Jonathan F. Woodside, Charles Madeira.

Carpenters—Conrad Christman, Frederick Fisher, Henry Johnson, Samuel Cook, James Bramble, William Waddle, John Pickens, Christopher Andricks, Richard Snyder, George Frew, Adam Reister, Thomas Bradford, Wesley Browning, Jesse Purdum, James Clark.

Saddlers—James McDougal, Thomas McDougal, Samuel

Ewing, Samuel C. Clifford, Peter Leister, Robert Long, Alexander Ewing.

Saddletree Makers—Daniel Dulaney, Joseph Sands.

Hatters—George Williams, ——— Farin, John Butler, John Laird, Hawks & Swift, Andrew McGinnis, Joseph Thompson, E. W. Smith.

Tinners—Henry Jack, William Jack, Andrew Deemer.

Whitesmiths—Jacob Ott, Daniel Ott, Michael Ott.

Tailors—John Watson, Alexander Beard, John Hall, John Hunter, Thomas Loyd, William D. Clarie, Jonas Baum, Moses Levi, William Y. Gilmore, James Montgomery, George Wolf, ——— Clark, John Mitchell, Joseph Kirkpatrick.

Groceries and Liquor Stores—Limle & Wolfe, Thomas Murray, Amasa Ives, John Rogers, Thomas Braden.

Gunsmiths—Peter Fortney, Isaac Groves, Jerman Jordan.

Stone and Brick Masons—Levi Sidwell, Hugh Black, Benjamin Thompson, John Watson, William Rutledge, Henry Summersett, James Gibbs, Peter Brown, John England, George Saxton, James Brown, Owen Dailey, Eleazer Dailey, Aaron Dailey.

Chair Makers—James Phillips, ——— Anderson, Thomas Renshaw, Henry May, Christopher Tucker, Hector Sandford, George Hoffman.

Wheelwrights—James Robinson, James Howard.

Potteries—George Snapp, Jacob Wolf.

Lumber Merchant—James English.

Painters—Daniel Madeira, William Stubbs, Joseph Dunlap.

Blacksmiths—Peter Day, George Haynes, George Scott, Edward Fitzgerald, George Hitchens, Hugh Hillhouse, Samuel Hillhouse, Adam Nebergall, Thomas S. Brattin, ——— Thompson, Jacob Bonser, Alexander Wibly.

Farmers—Anthony Walke, Joseph Kerr, James Swearengen, John Johnson.

Shoe Stores—Drayton M. Curtis, E. P. Kendrick.

Boot and Shoe Makers—William Mayhew, John McCormick, John Dun, Solomon Curtis, ——— Saxton, Jacob May,

Michael Byerly, Ezekiel Knowles, William Knowles, James Ryan, John Ross, George W. Chandley.

Pump Makers—Jacob Eikleburner, George Motter.

Teamsters—Ely Harrison, Batteal Harrison, William Watt, Joseph Farden, Andrew Poe, John Armstrong.

Grocery and Clothing Store—William H. Leffingwell.

Dyer—Barnett Lauman.

Butchers—Matthias Hufnagle, Daniel McCollister, Conrad Fultz, John Briney, John Baker, Daniel Baker, Zebulon Hukle.

Bakers—Adam Haller, John Martin, William Cogan, John Hutt, Lawrence McClure, William Davidson, John Clifford.

Brewers—William Robbins, Abram Kopp, John W. Collett, —— Donahue.

Rope Factory—Johnson Lofland.

Well Digger—Peter Briney.

Of all those named above but twenty-eight are now living.

General Duncan McArthur.

[From Howe's Historical Collections of Ohio.]

Near Adena, in a beautiful situation, is Fruit Hill, the seat of the late General Duncan McArthur, and latterly the residence of his son-in-law, the Hon. Wm. Allen.

Duncan McArthur, who was of Scotch parentage, was born in Dutchess county, New York, in 1772, and when eight years of age his father moved to the frontiers of Pennsylvania. His father was in indigent circumstances, and Duncan, when of sufficient age, hired out as a laborer. At the age of eighteen years, he was a volunteer in Harmar's campaign. In 1792, he was a private in the company of Captain William Enoch, and acted with so much intrepidity in the battle of Captina as to render him very popular with the frontier men. After this, he was for awhile a laborer at some salt works near Maysville, Kentucky, and in the spring of 1793 engaged as a chain-bearer to General Nathaniel Massie, and penetrated with him and others into the Scioto Valley to make surveys, at a time when such an enterprise was full of danger from the Indians. He was afterward employed as a spy against the Indians on the Ohio, and had some adventures with them, elsewhere detailed in this volume. He was again in the employment of General Massie; and after the treaty of Greenville, studied surveying, became an assistant surveyor to General Massie, and aided him to lay out Chillicothe. He, in the course of this business, became engaged in the purchase and sale of lands, by which he acquired great landed wealth.

In 1805, he was a member of the legislature from Ross; in 1806, elected colonel, and in 1808, major general of the State militia. In May, 1812, he was commissioned colonel in the Ohio Volunteers, afterward marched to Detroit, and himself and regiment were included in Hull's surrender. He was second in command on this unfortunate expedition; but such was the energy he displayed, that, notwithstanding, after his return as a prisoner of war on parole, the Democratic party, in the fall of 1812, elected him to Congress by an overwhelming majority. In March, 1813, he was commissioned a brigadier general in the army, and having been regularly exchanged as prisoner of war, soon after resigned his seat in Congress to engage in active service.

About the time the enemy were preparing to attack Fort Stevenson, the frontiers were in great danger, and Harrison sent an express to McArthur to hurry on to the scene of action with all the force he could muster. Upon this, he ordered the second division to march in mass.

This march of the militia was named the "*general call.*" As soon as Governor Meigs was advised of the call made by McArthur, he went forward and assumed in person the command of the militia now under arms. General McArthur went forward to the scene of action, and the militia followed in thousands. So promptly were his orders obeyed, that in a few days the Sandusky plains were covered with nearly eight thousand men, mostly from Scioto Valley. This rush of militia to defend the exposed frontier of our country bore honorable testimony that the patriotism of the citizens of the Scioto Valley did not consist of noisy professions, but of practical service in defense of their country. This general turn-out of the militia proves that General Massie, and the few pioneers who followed him into the wilderness and assisted him in making the first settlements in the fertile valley of the Scioto river, had infused their own daring and enterprising spirit into the spirit of the community. Among these eight thousand militia were found in the ranks, as private soldiers, judges, merchants, lawyers, preachers, doctors, mechanics, farmers, and laborers of every description—all anxious to repulse the ruthless invaders of our soil. Indeed, the Scioto country was so stripped of its male population on this occasion, that the women, in their absence, were compelled to carry their grain to mill or let their children suffer from want. These troops having arrived at Upper Sandusky formed what was called the " grand camp of Ohio militia." General McArthur was detailed to the command of Fort Meigs. The victory of Perry, on the 10th of September, gave a fresh impetus to the army, and Harrison concentrated his troops at Portage river, where, on the 20th, the brigade of McArthur, from Fort Meigs, joined him. On the 27th, the army embarked in boats, and crossed over to Malden, and a few days after, General McArthur, with the greater part of the troops, was charged with the defense of Detroit.

After the resignation of Harrison, in the spring of 1814, McArthur, being the senior brigadier general, the command of the Northwestern army devolved on him. As the enemy retired discomfited from the upper end of Lake Erie, and most of the Indians were suing for peace, the greater part of the regular troops under his command were ordered to the Niagara frontier. McArthur had a number of small forts to garrison along the frontier, while he kept his main force at Detroit and Malden to overawe the Canadians and the scattering Indians still in the British interest. The dull monotony of going from post to post was not the most agreeable service to his energetic mind. He projected an expedition into Canada, on which he was absent about a fortnight from Detroit, with six hundred and fifty troops and seventy Indians. At or near Malcolm's Mill, the detachment had an action with a force of about five hundred Canadian militia, in which they defeated them with a loss of twenty-seven killed and wounded, and made one hundred and eleven prisoners ; while the American loss was only one killed and six wounded. In this excursion, the valuable mills of the enemy, in the vicinity of Grand river, were destroyed, and their resources in that quarter essentially impaired. After returning from this successful expedition, the war languished in the Northwest. General McArthur continued in service, and was at Detroit when peace was declared.

In the fall of 1815, he was again elected to the legislature. In 1816, he was appointed commissioner to negotiate a treaty with the Indians at Springwell, near Detroit; he acted in the same capacity at the treaty of Fort Meigs, in September, 1817, and also at the treaty at St. Mary's, in the succeeding year. In 1817, upon being elected to the legislature, he was a competitor with the late Charles Hammond, Esq., for the speaker's chair, and triumphed by a small majority, The next summer the party strife on the United States' Bank question, which had commenced the previous session, was violent. McArthur defended the right of that institution to place branches wherever it chose in the State, and on this issue was again a candidate for the legislature and was defeated.

A considerable majority of members elected this year were opposed to the United States' Bank. Mr. Hammond was again elected a member of the Assembly, and by his talents, and readiness in wielding his pen, together with his strong and confident manner of speaking, was able to dictate law to this Assembly. A law was passed at this session of the legislature, taxing each branch of the United States' Bank, located in the State of Ohio, fifty thousand dollars. When the time arrived for collecting this tax, the branch banks refused to pay.

Mr. Hammond had provided in the law for a case of this kind ; the collector, with an armed force, entered the branch bank in the town of Chillicothe and took what money he thought proper.

" The bank brought suit in the United States Circuit Court against all the State officers concerned in this forcible collection. Mr. Hammond, a distinguished lawyer, with other eminent counsel, were employed by the State of Ohio to defend this important cause. The District Court decided the law of Ohio, levying the tax, unconstitutional, and, of course, null and void ; and made a decree, directing the State to refund to the bank the money thus forcibly taken. The cause was appealed to the Supreme Court of the United States. Mr. Hammond defended the suit in all its stages. The Supreme Court decided this cause against the State of Ohio. Thus was settled this knotty and vexatious question, which, for a time, threatened the peace of the Union."

In 1819, McArthur was again elected to the legislature. In 1822, he was again chosen to Congress, and became an undeviating supporter of what was then called the American system. While General McArthur remained a member of Congress, he had considerable influence in that body. His persevering industry, his energetic mind, his sound judgment, and practical business habits, rendered him a very efficient member. He would sometimes make short, pithy remarks on the business of the house, but made no attempts at those flourishes of eloquence which tickle the fancy and please the ear. After having served two sessions in Congress, he declined a re-election, being determined to devote all his efforts to arrange his domestic concerns. He left the field of politics to others, and engaged with unremitting attention to settle his land business.

In 1830, McArthur was elected Governor of Ohio by the anti-Jackson party, and on the expiration of his term of office was a candidate for Congress, and lost his election, which terminated his political career. By an unfortunate accident, in

June, 1830, McArthur was horribly bruised and maimed. From this severe misfortune his bodily and mental powers constantly declined, until death, several years after, closed his career.

Duncan McArthur was a strong minded, energetic man, and possessed an iron will. He was an honorable man, close in business, and had many bitter and severe enemies. His life adds another to the many examples of the workings of our free institutions, of one rising from obscurity to the highest offices in the gift of a State.

Thomas Worthington—Chronological Sketch.

1773. Thomas Worthington, youngest son of Robert Worthington, was born near Charleston, Jefferson (then Berkeley) county, Virginia.

Robert Worthington, a farmer, was a man of great energy and industry; a justice of the peace, and afterward a captain of scouts during the French and Indian war of 1755.

1780. Lost both his parents, and his early education neglected.

1786. Chose for his guardian General William Darke, and then, for the first time is sent regularly to school, and kindly treated.

General Darke was a captain in the Virginia line during the Revolutionary war, and a rough old Indian fighter afterward; was present at St. Clair's defeat. He was very kind to his ward, and sent him to the best schools (not very good) that the country then afforded, and endeavored to procure him a midshipman's warrant to gratify his longing for the sea, but did not succeed. One of his sons accompanied Thomas Worthington to Georgetown, where he enlisted as a sailor.

1790. Goes to sea, contrary to the wishes of his guardian, as a common sailor, in the Brittania. a British merchant vessel, of Port Greenock, Scotland.

1790-91. Visits (as a sailor) the northern parts of the British Islands, and many of the ports of Denmark, Sweden, Norway, and Russia. Remains absent two years.

1792. Narrowly escapes being impressed as a sailor by a

British press-gang. Grows tired of the life of a sailor, and returns home.

A press-gang came aboard the vessel at Port Greenock. All hands were paraded on deck, and, probably in compliment to his good looks, our young American was selected to serve the king. He was claimed as a British subject, and a deserter from a British man of war. These *facts* were proved by competent false witnesses to the entire satisfaction of the red-nosed lieutenant who commanded the press-gang, and he was about to take possession of his hopeful recruit—stout, well made, and just six feet high—quite a prize. At this juncture James Taylor, captain of the vessel, and a true friend of young Worthington, took the leader of the press-gang aside, and told him that the relatives and guardian of Worthington were persons of wealth and influence in Virginia, who would not fail to institute inquiries about him, which would be very damaging to any one who should violate his rights as an American citizen. These statements, and a small fee, turned the scales, and Worthington escaped the direful slavery of a British man of war, to which so many of our countrymen were then, and for years afterward, subjected. He was always grateful to the generous Englishman who saved him from this cruel bondage, and a friendly correspondence was kept up between them for many years.

1796. Married to Eleanor Swearingen, and visits the then Northwest Territory, examines it, and (1797) purchases land near Chillicothe.

Eleanor, wife of Thomas Worthington, was a woman of fine mind and culture and remarkable business capacity. Delicately brought up, she faced the dangers and hardships of the new settlement in the Northwest Territory with a brave spirit. Her husband being mostly in public life, she managed his property in his absence with great skill and success. She was left a widow in 1827, with ten children, and a large estate deeply incumbered with debt. She contributed greatly, by her economy, frugality, and self-denial, to the education of the younger children, and, by her wise counsels, secured to them all a large part of their inheritance. She died in 1849, at a good old age, with the blessings of the many afflicted whom her active charities had relieved, and beloved and respected by all.

1798. April. Removes, with his wife and an infant daughter, to Chillicothe, having liberated with her consent and brought with them to the free Northwest Territory, her slaves and his own, forty-six in number, of all ages and of both sexes. Builds mill, plants orchards, and clears land.

1799-1801. Member of the Territorial Legislature.

1802. Member of the Constitutional Convention.

While the first Constitutional Convention of Ohio was in session, Mr. Worthington learned from a hunter whom he confided in, that the "Southern bend" of Lake Michigan was "a day's journey" further south than represented on the maps of the day. He therefore introduced the clause which eventually secured to Ohio the mouth of the Maumee river and the sites of Toledo and Maumee, with a strip of valuable territory. He also introduced a clause prohibiting negro apprenticeships, and thus prevented in Ohio a form of negro slavery which prevailed for many years in Indiana and Illinois.

1803-07 and 1810-14. Member of the Senate of the United States.

While in the United States Senate, he procured the passage of a law dividing the public domain into quarter sections instead of squares of two miles; also, Worthington's law for quieting land titles in the Virginia Military District, well known and much approved by the settlers of the day.

1815-19. Governor of Ohio; founded the Ohio State Library.

Soon after his election as Governor, while on a visit to Columbus, he saw that the public square on which the Capitol now stands was in a rude and filthy condition, and incumbered with logs and brush piles. The town authorities would do nothing, so he went to the warden of the Penitentiary and induced him to give him the control of about thirty of the convicts, with the necessary guards. After a brief speech to this squad, he marched them to the public square, and, for two days, kept them busily at work, sharing their labors, until the square was entirely cleared. No man attempted to escape, and all worked cheerfully and efficiently. This anecdote I had from the late Dr. Lincoln Goodale, who was present and witnessed the joint labor, for the public good, of the Governor and convicts.

1820-25. In the Ohio Legislature; took a prominent part in the new systems of finance and of common schools, the Ohio canal, the penitentiary system, etc.

To his adopted State the labors of Thomas Worthington during these latter years of his life were the most valuable of all. Then was laid the foundations of the prosperity and progress for which Ohio has since been so remarkable. And in this great work there was no man who labored more faithfully and efficiently than he did, in shaping the new systems of finance, public instruction, and public improvements then commenced.

1826. Canal Commissioner.

1827—June 20. Died at the city of New York.

Hon. William Allen.

William Allen, the subject of this brief record, is truly a self-made man. He emigrated from Virginia to Chillicothe at an early day, on foot and alone—a boy. He was sent by a relative to the Chillicothe Academy, where he soon developed, as a member of the debating society, talents of the first order, and early attracted the attention of the leading men of Chillicothe. Finishing his studies, he was induced by friends to study law with General Edward King, an eminent attorney. He graduated with high distinction, and became celebrated as an orator. Colonel Allen represented the Chillicothe district in Congress for one term, and as a Senator of Ohio for two terms. He was the acknowledged leader of his party. He married the daughter of the late Governor McArthur, and is the owner of the celebrated Fruit Hill farm. Dr. Scott, his son-in-law, lives with him.

Early Settlers.

Rev. Hector Sanford emigrated to the Scioto Valley in 1799, and was one of the first ministers in Chillicothe. His father, Angus Sanford, came from England in 1772, and served as an officer in the Revolutionary war; was also with Dunmore in 1774. Hector's sons are Joseph, John, and Lemuel. Major John Willet was in the war of 1812; was an early pioneer and a brave man. General McNeary was in the war of 1812; his old homestead still stands on McNeary's run.

The following names of early settlers were contributed by John Robinson : William Rogers, Andrew and George Pontious, Peter Porter, James, Robert, Joseph, Jacob, and William McDill, Michael Thomas, Robert Adams, James McCrae, Joseph Clark, William Robinson, Enos and John Pursell, Jacob Grundy, Richard and John Acton, Thomas, Robert, and William Brown, William Pool, James Danans, John and George Ricups,

Daniel Dixon, Robert Worthington, Thomas Shields, James Prior, Hugh and James Cochran, Samuel Smith, Daniel Augustus, James Carr, James Armstrong, Thomas Earl, Thomas Junk, John Haynes ; Thomas Arthur, still living, and ninety years of age. All the above were early pioneers of West Scioto township.

Nicholas Haynes, father of Henry and John Haynes—who are still living on the old homestead—emigrated to West Scioto in 1808. He was in the Revolutionary war. The Haynes family record shows thirty names between 1769 and 1815.

James Shane, one of the pioneers, was a Dunkard preacher, and a noted hunter in early times, and had two sons—Daniel and Abraham. He occupied part of the farm known as the Wood's tract. Hugh and Alonzo Carson and the Sullivan family were the first men in the valley. The Dunn family were also among the earliest pioneers. E. Fullerton was a squatter on the old Zane tract, and an active defender of the settlement against Indian attacks. The old Zane trace passed through this section on the east side of the river. Isaac, Jacob, Andrew, and Adam Creamer settled near the river. Adam was in the Revolution under General Greene, and all of his boys were in the war of 1812 under General Harrison. They were all strong, hearty, large men, well calculated to endure the hardships and privations of pioneer life. Many of their descendants now live in Fayette county.

Colored Pioneers.

Thomas Watson came in 1796; Henry Evens, 1798; Robert Pleasant, 179?; Nelson Piles, 1800; Samuel Nichol, 1808; Abram Nichol, 1809; Peter James, 1812; Henry Hill, 1813; John Fidler, Ser.., 1814; John Fidler, Jr., 1814. The above settled in Scioto township.

Indian Occupation of Ross County in 1750.

The Shawanese, Piquas, and Chillicothe tribes.

Main Street.

B. Gorham, merchant tailor; William Hays, baker; John Ewing, grocer; Jeremiah McCollister, wholesale liquor merchant; Adam Greisheimer, huckster and grocer; John Kellhofer, stove and tin store; Thomas Murphy, grocer; William Conner, grocer; S. H. Mosher, grocer; H. W. Woodrow, sewing machines; John Gunther, grocer; William Vincent, grocer; B. F. Duncan, Singer machine agent; E. K. Mick, auctioneer; E. F. Lewis, saddler; A. W. West, gunsmith; John Dunn, marble works; Jacob Buchen, dry goods.

Paint Street.

R. B. Smart, T. Woodrow, Clough & Bennett, Carson & Budd, S. C. Swift, F. Hellman, Joseph Stewart, Peter Hoffman, Carlisle & Co., A. H. Warner, dry goods merchants; Dr. R. H. Lansing, John A. Nipgen, Allston & Davis, druggists; J. G. Snyder, M. Lewis & Co., wholesale hardware stores; A. C. Ireland, wholesale stove and tin store; C. C. Limle, stove and copper shop; C. Erdman, D. Kline, S. Epstine, H. Heicht, J. Jurenmou, clothing stores; P. M. Miner, Miller Patterson & Cutter, hat stores; C. F. Dufeu, Anton Pfaff, S. Shreckengaust, jewelers; W. E. Buser, furniture store; Emmett House, Warner House, Union House; John Kaiser, F. Marluff, confectioners; Platter, Claypool & Ingall, wholesale grocers; William Jacob, I. Cory, Smart & Kilvert, grocers; M. Cahill, M. N. Hurst, J. G. Weidman, shoe stores; Schaeffer & Kramer, E. H. Kauffman, tobacconists; G. W. White, F. A. Simonds, photographers; G. W. Harper, bazar; St. Burkley, music store; A. Pearson, A. Mottz, saddlers; W. B. Mills, painter and glazier; Mrs. E. Mead, milliner; E. P. Safford, G. P. Schaeffer, insurance agents; J. H. Putnam, *Advertiser;* Bond & Son, *Gazette;* Armstrong, *Register;* James Rowe, United States land office receiver; W. B. Franklin, United States register; Hugh McCorry, provisions, groceries, etc.; Maule & Elsass, dry goods; T. & M. Schilder, J. Sully, grocers.

Water Street.

Barmann & Burgess, dry goods store; Clark & Boggs, wholesale grocers; Wm. Poland, wholesale liquor and grocer; Boulger & Co., wholesale liquor merchants; Bartlett & Son, wholesale packers, etc.; E. Lewis, druggist; J. T. Bonner, flour and feed store; Marfield & Bro., Clinton Mills; Bennett & Co., J. Hirn, grocers; J. R. Bailey, baker and grocer; P. Fink, meat shop; T. J. Guin, steam stone mill; A. J. Barlow, livery and feed stable; Frank Reppel, furniture store; M. Brendle, shoe store; Schrader & Betz, carriage manufactory; Miss Briggs, milliner; Clinton House; G. A. Benner, Mrs. Hanley, J. Hirn, clothiers, etc.; Baber House; J. F. Woodsides, Ætna sewing factory; H. M. Pinto, insurance agent; A. Helmuth, grocer; F. Aid, shoe shop; Chillicothe House, A. Hirn; D. Oberer, saddler.

Walnut Street.

J. Brown, wagon shop; J. W. Brown, cigar factory; C. E. Rosenfeld, furniture and picture frame factory; W. B. Haynes, gunsmith; G. Gesler, baker; Assor Blackburn, blacksmith; Lewis Shenkle, furniture store.

Second Street.

G. J. Herman, dry goods; Schrader & Betz, carriage manufactory; G. W. Fitzsimmons, R. G. Duff, W. A. Ziebold, J. R. Deiter, Hugh Savage, grocers; H. Maul, merchant tailor; Yeo & Son, G. Perkins, books and stationery; Philip Kline, leather store; L. Molenkophf, book bindery; Welsh & Son, foundery; Phœnix House; J. Snyder, wood and coal yard; D. Thompson, livery; James Ewing, livery and feed stable; Hollenhopher, shoe store; post-office, C. Brown, P. M.; Dr. H. W. How, operative and mechanical dentist, Kaiser's block, second story; Jackson Bouser, wagon and carriage shop; Baker & Son, meat shop; A. Fiddler, livery establishment; Mills & Huffman, furniture and chairs; D. Montgomery, notions; John Howard, undertaker; J. F. Cook, architect.

Professional Business Men.

C. E. Brown, Vanmeter & Neal, Thomas Kelly, W. A. Gage, attorneys at law, Second street; Mayo & Du Hadway, Milton L. Clark, C. Wm. Gilmore, J. C. Entrikin, Thomas Worthington, Beach & Lawrence, J. H. Keith, attorneys, Paint street; Drs. Waddle, Scearce and Miesse, C. H. French, Second street; Dr. J. M. Wiltshire, Fifth street; Dr. J. Miller, Main street; Drs. Hubble, G. S. Franklin, Paint street; Judge Safford, office court house; U. S. Claypool, attorney, Londary; Dr. D. A. Miller, Roxabell; Samuel L. Wallace, attorney, Second street; McClintick & Smith, attorneys, Second street; Minshall & Throckmorton, attorneys, Main and Paint streets; Dr. D. V. Grace, veterinary surgeon, Union House, Paint street.

Officers of Ross County.

Sheriff, John S. Mace; Auditor, Saml. Kendrick; Treasurer, Wm. A. Wayland; Recorder, Wm. Briggs; Clerk, P. G. Griffin; Probate Judge, Thos. Walke; Prosecuting Attorney, L. T. Neal; Commissioners, Saml. Cline, Saml. Nichol, Wesley Claypool.

www.ingramcontent.com/pod-product-compliance
Lightning Source LLC
Chambersburg PA
CBHW030601270326
41927CB00007B/1008